GUILTY SECRET

Roger Mortimer-Smith

GUILTY SECRET

A thriller in two acts

OBERON BOOKS
LONDON

WWW.OBERONBOOKS.COM

First published in 2012 by Oberon Books Ltd
521 Caledonian Road, London N7 9RH
Tel: +44 (0) 20 7607 3637 / Fax: +44 (0) 20 7607 3629
e-mail: info@oberonbooks.com
www.oberonbooks.com

A catalogue record for this book is available from the British
Library.

ISBN: 978-1-84943-202-3

Cover design by James Illman

To Clare, the glamorous socialist

To Raffles, the gentleman thief

To Gordon, for putting up with a bolshy little sod

And to Nadine, the rasta diva

Characters

GEORGE
40s, speaks with a detectable East-End accent
but very cultivated and controlled

LENNIE
early 20s, speaks with a rougher East-End accent

CHARLOTTE
mid 20s, attractive and well groomed,
clearly high maintenance, speaks with an
upper-class accent

CRICHTON
40s, calm and deliberate in his movements
and speech

Guilty Secret was first performed at The Mill at Sonning on 9th June 2011 with the following cast:

GEORGE – Jeffrey Holland

LENNIE – Neil Andrew

CHARLOTTE – Katie Beard

CRICHTON – Philip Childs

Directed by Anthony Valentine

Set designed by Dinah England

Costumes designed by Jane Kidd

Lighting designed by Matthew Biss

Act One

The living room of an isolated farmhouse. It is a holiday cottage out of season, and has a slightly shabby and neglected air. Front door and windows stage right, door to kitchen stage left. Another door in the back wall which presumably leads to the rest of the house. In the room are a sofa, an armchair, a coffee table and a side table with a cordless telephone on it.

To begin with it is dark, though there is just enough natural light for us to make out what is happening. We hear the sound of a car approaching. GEORGE enters from the door in the back wall, dressed in an overcoat and wearing gloves, and goes to the window. He takes out a digital camera from his coat pocket. As the headlights of the car sweep the room, he takes a picture out of the window, which he then examines on the camera's screen. Satisfied, he puts the camera back in his pocket and sits down. Meanwhile the car has come to a stop and we hear the engine turn off and the door open and close. Footsteps. A key turns in the lock. LENNIE enters, similarly dressed. He finds the light switch, turns it on and sees GEORGE.

LENNIE: *(Startled.)* Bloody 'ell! You nearly gave me an 'eart attack!

GEORGE: Sorry Lennie. I didn't mean to startle you.

LENNIE: I thought you wasn't here yet.

GEORGE: Sorry, I should have turned the lights on. Thoughtless of me.

LENNIE: *(Closing the door.)* What are you sitting there in the dark for anyway?

GEORGE: *(Pointedly.)* Secrecy, Len. Secrecy is crucial to the success of the whole operation.

For a moment LENNIE is baffled by this, but shrugs it off.

LENNIE: You found it alright, anyway?

GEORGE: Yeah, no problems. Your directions were excellent.

LENNIE: So what d'you reckon to it?

GEORGE: Perfect. Right in the middle of nowhere. Couldn't be better.

LENNIE is visibly proud at being praised. GEORGE stands.

GEORGE: And the room itself, so…anonymous.

LENNIE: Eh?

GEORGE: I'm saying it's got no distinguishing features to make it memorable, or give you a clue where it is. A sofa, a chair, a table. Could be just about anywhere in the world.

LENNIE: *(Eagerly.)* 'Cept Japan. They ain't got chairs there. They sit right on the floor.

GEORGE looks at him.

LENNIE: I saw this film.

GEORGE: Well, I think they have chairs these days, Lennie. The film you saw must have been set in the past. In feudal Japan.

LENNIE: Yeah, tha's what it was all about. There was this big feud between these two…samurais or ninjas or sumfin'. You seen it an' all?

GEORGE: No, feudal means… I'm saying it must have been set hundreds of years ago.

LENNIE considers.

LENNIE: Naah, couldn't have been. They couldn't make films then, could they? *(Amused.)* Fancy you not knowin' that!

GEORGE: Never mind. How long have we got this place for anyway?

LENNIE: A week.

GEORGE: *(Taken aback.)* A week? I sincerely hope it doesn't take that long.

LENNIE: They wouldn't do it for less than a week.

GEORGE: Well, no matter. What's a little extra expense in the grand scheme of things?

GEORGE pulls his coat around him.

GEORGE: Bit bleedin' chilly though, isn't it?

LENNIE: I did turn the heatin' on earlier. 'Spose it just takes a while to warm up. I don't think anyone's been here for a while.

GEORGE: I can't say I blame them. Everything go OK at your end?

LENNIE: Yeah, fine. No problems.

GEORGE: You waited 20 minutes like I said?

LENNIE: Yeah. *(Slight pause.)* I didn't really get why, though.

GEORGE: Just to be on the safe side.

LENNIE tries to puzzle this out, but gets nowhere and gives up.

GEORGE: You're sure no one saw you?

LENNIE: No.

GEORGE: No, no one saw you, or no, you're not sure?

LENNIE: Yeah.

GEORGE: *(With infinite patience.)* Lennie, is there any chance that anyone saw you?

Beat.

LENNIE: When?

GEORGE: *(Through gritted teeth.)* In the car park.

LENNIE: Oh, right. No. Don't think so anyway.

GEORGE: I hope you're right. *(He looks at his watch, then walks to the window.)* It gets properly dark out here, doesn't it? Not like in town. It's all just a little bit unnerving.

LENNIE: I was looking at the stars just now, before I came in. I couldn't believe how many there are out here. *(Slight pause.)* But then I thought, there must be the same number wherever you are. I mean, even though it seems like a long drive, 'specially if there's traffic, compared to the distance to the stars iss like nuffin' at all. So even if you've driven for, like, hours, it don't make no difference to how many stars there are. You just can't see 'em in town.

GEORGE: *(Drily.)* Yes, Lennie.

LENNIE: Cos of the light from houses and lamp posts and that.

GEORGE: I think I understand the principle, thank you.

Beat.

LENNIE: *(Excited.)* Do you really think it's gonna work this time?

GEORGE: I don't see why it shouldn't. Thorough planning's the key to these things, planning for every possible eventuality.

LENNIE: *(Happily.)* Iss gonna be great bein' rich. I keep thinkin' about what I'm gonna do with my share. I got loads of ideas. Do you know what you're gonna do, Mr Reynolds?

GEORGE: *(Turning angrily.)* Lennie!

LENNIE: Sorry, I mean... George.

GEORGE: We've been over this a million times.

LENNIE: Yeah, I know. I'm sorry.

GEORGE: We only get one chance at this. If you screw this up...

LENNIE: I won't, I promise.

GEORGE: You do understand why it's important, don't you?

LENNIE: Yeah, 'course I do.

Beat.

LENNIE: *(Hesitantly.)* Only...

GEORGE: *(Sharply.)* What?

Beat.

LENNIE: *(Discouraged.)* Doesn't matter.

GEORGE: Ask me, Lennie. *(Calmer.)* Look, I'm sorry I was angry just now. I'm just a bit tense, that's all. But if there's something you want to know, just ask me, OK? It's important we both go into this knowing what we're doing.

LENNIE: OK…it's just that… I don't get why I have to call you George when she's not here.

GEORGE: *(Placatory.)* Now that's a perfectly reasonable question. And the reason is that the more we call each other by these names, the more natural they'll feel to us, and that makes it less likely we'll slip up when she *is* here. You understand?

LENNIE: Yeah.

GEORGE: If I had any sense, I'd have made you call me George for the last couple of weeks, just to make sure it got drummed in properly.

LENNIE: Oh you got loadsa sense, Mr…

GEORGE turns sharply, LENNIE catches himself in time.

LENNIE: …George. You got enough sense for the both of us.

GEORGE: *(Under his breath.)* I can only hope.

LENNIE: So you're not angry no more?

GEORGE: No, it's fine. No harm done.

LENNIE: I am sorry. I'll be really careful from now on.

GEORGE: Don't worry about it. You're only human. *(Slight pause.)* If it makes you feel better, I've just realised I've made a bit of a cock up myself.

LENNIE: *(Surprised.)* Yeah?

GEORGE gets his phone out of his pocket.

GEORGE: My mobile. Should have known I wouldn't get a signal out here.

He puts the phone away.

LENNIE: I got a new mobile a while back.

GEORGE: *(Not interested.)* Yeah?

LENNIE: Me old one wasn't broken or nuffin', I just wanted a new one. I like to get a new model every year. I 'ad this idea. I'd sell me old phone for a lot of money, and buy a new phone for not much money. That way I'd end up with a better phone, and more money.

GEORGE looks at him.

GEORGE: *(Drily.)* Funny how brilliant ideas always seem so obvious once someone else has thought of them...

LENNIE: Didn't work though.

GEORGE: *(Seemingly amazed.)* No...really?

LENNIE: I couldn't get as much for me old phone as the new one cost.

GEORGE: Ah well, the best laid plans of...er...whatever it is. Have you got it with you?

LENNIE: What?

GEORGE: *(Patiently.)* Your mobile. You might have a signal if you're on a different network.

LENNIE: Naah. Charging up at home, isn't it?

GEORGE: *(Surprised.)* Don't you take it with you when you go out?

LENNIE: I used to, but it runs down the battery.

GEORGE considers this for a moment, but decides against pursuing it.

GEORGE: Never mind, there's a landline we can use.

He lifts the receiver to check for a dial tone.

GEORGE: It's fine. Well, I think we're about ready for the off. Lennie?

LENNIE does not respond.

GEORGE: *(More forcefully.)* Lennie!

LENNIE: *(Suddenly.)* Oh yeah, sorry. I forgot Lennie was me.

GEORGE: Even so, there's no one else here, is there? Jesus wept.

LENNIE: *(Embarrassed.)* Sorry.

GEORGE: Anyway, I was going to ask if you wanted to go before we start.

LENNIE: Where?

GEORGE: *(Patiently.)* The toilet, Lennie.

LENNIE: No, I'm alright.

GEORGE: You sure? There might not be a chance later. So speak now or forever hold your piss.

LENNIE: I'm sure.

GEORGE: OK then. You got the gun I gave you?

LENNIE opens his coat to show him the gun tucked into his waistband.

GEORGE: Bloody hell, Len, I hope you've checked the safety catch is on. There are some things money can't replace.

LENNIE: Yeah, thassa thought.

LENNIE gets the gun out, checks the safety catch and tucks it back in his waistband.

LENNIE: You want me to go and get her now?

GEORGE: In a moment, Len. Isn't there something else we need to do first?

LENNIE thinks, but doesn't come up with anything.

GEORGE: Why do you think I gave you that balaclava? *(LENNIE seems perplexed.)* Ski mask. You have to put it on first. Did you forget?

LENNIE: No, I didn't forget. It's just… I bin thinkin' about that.

GEORGE: *(With infinite patience.)* Oh good.

LENNIE: What it is, right, I don't reckon she'd remember me anyway.

GEORGE: *(Drily.)* You don't think she might guess that the man getting her out of the boot of her car is probably the same man who locked her in it in the first place?

LENNIE: *(Oblivious to the sarcasm.)* Yeah, she'll prob'ly guess that. I mean, she won't reco'nise me from *before.* I bin around a lot of people like that, and the thing is, if you're not one of their sort, they just look straight through you. Like you wasn't even there.

GEORGE: Lennie, the balaclava isn't to prevent her recognising you *now*. As you say, she probably wouldn't. It's so that she can't describe you to the police *later*.

LENNIE: Oh, right. *(Considers.)* Yeah, thassa good idea.

GEORGE: You're very kind. So, put it on, please, then off you go.

LENNIE fishes in his pockets for his balaclava.

GEORGE: *(Concerned.)* You did have it on earlier, though? When you grabbed her?

LENNIE: I was goin' to. But then I thought, people don't normally walk around in a car park wearin' a baklava, do they? It'd look suspicious.

GEORGE: Fair point. Just as long as she didn't see your face.

LENNIE: Don't worry. Came up from behind, didn't I? Gave her the old bodyform over the mouth and we were away.

GEORGE: Chloroform, you mean. At least, I sincerely hope you do.

LENNIE: Yeah, tha's the one.

Balaclava now on, LENNIE goes out through the back door. GEORGE watches him go, and rolls his eyes.

GEORGE: Never work with children or animals...

GEORGE takes his own balaclava out of his coat pocket and puts it on. We hear the sound of the car boot opening and closing. LENNIE returns carrying CHARLOTTE in his arms. Her hands are tied in front of her, her feet are tied together and she is gagged.

LENNIE: On the sofa?

GEORGE: If you'd be so kind.

LENNIE puts CHARLOTTE down on the sofa. At the last moment she grabs at him and, before he can prevent it, wrenches the balaclava off his head.

GEORGE: *(Furious.)* Lennie!

LENNIE: *(Panicked.)* Iss not my fault!

GEORGE: I told you to tie her hands up!

LENNIE: I did!

GEORGE: Behind her back, you stupid bastard! Do I have to spell every last little thing out for you? Jesus Christ.

He paces angrily around the room.

LENNIE: *(Defensively.)* I just thought…

GEORGE stops pacing.

GEORGE: *(Angrily.)* What? What did you think, Lennie? Do please share this pearl of wisdom with us. I'm only sorry the Nobel Prize committee isn't here to hear it for themselves.

Beat.

LENNIE: I thought it might hurt. After a while.

GEORGE: *(Incredulous.)* What did you say?!?

LENNIE: If her hands were tied behind her back. I thought…

GEORGE: *(Acidly.)* Oh, you thought that, did you? Well wasn't that considerate of you. If ever Miss Chamberlain decides to write a Good Kidnappers Guide, I'm sure you'll get the full five stars for courtesy and thoughtfulness. In the meantime, you've landed us right up shit creek.

He resumes pacing.

GEORGE: What did I say to you? One mistake, that's all it would take. But I didn't imagine even you would screw it up before we'd even started.

GEORGE takes off his own balaclava.

LENNIE: *(Alarmed.)* Well don't take yours off an all!

GEORGE: *(Angrily.)* There's no point in me keeping it on now, is there? She can identify you, and the police can trace the connection between us. We are, in the time-honoured phrase, 'known associates'. So, much as I wish it were otherwise, your stupidity has landed us both in it.

Beat. GEORGE sits down in the armchair again.

LENNIE: *(Frightened.)* I'm sorry.

GEORGE: *(Acidly.)* Oh, well that's alright then, just so long as you're sorry. That fixes everything, doesn't it? You may have plenty of time to reflect on how sorry you are in a small tiled room with nothing but a bunk bed and a bucket to piss in. And God help me, I'll probably be there with you. Or rather, God help you if I am.

Beat. LENNIE is too frightened to speak. GEORGE rubs his face and runs his fingers through his hair.

GEORGE: *(Calmer.)* Though I must admit, in some ways it is a relief.

LENNIE: *(Encouraged by his gentler tone.)* Yeah?

GEORGE: I can't stand wool next to my skin.

LENNIE: Yeah, it was a bit itchy.

GEORGE: I should probably have put them through the wash a couple of times. But these are brand new. Just got them yesterday.

LENNIE: Oh well. We'll know for next time.

GEORGE looks at LENNIE in astonishment, and despite himself he laughs at the absurdity of it all. LENNIE is encouraged by this.

GEORGE: Oh Lennie, they didn't make two of you, did they?

LENNIE: *(Puzzled by the question.)* Well, I've got a sister, but she's older. *(Conspiratorially.)* So what we gonna do about *(Inclines head to indicate CHARLOTTE.)* h-e-r?

GEORGE: *(Drily.)* Lennie, she was educated at Roedean, one of the best schools in the country. I think she can probably spell simple words.

CHARLOTTE reacts visibly to his knowing this about her.

LENNIE: Oh. Yeah.

Beat. GEORGE exhales audibly.

GEORGE: As to what we'll do, I honestly don't know. I need time to think. We'll just have to cross that bridge when we come to it.

Beat.

GEORGE: In the meantime, we seem to be neglecting our guest. Let's not add being poor hosts to our crimes. *(He turns to CHARLOTTE.)* Miss Chamberlain, allow me to welcome you to our abode, be it ever so humble. As you've probably gathered, my name's George, he's Lennie, and we'll be your kidnappers for the evening.

He checks his watch again.

GEORGE: Well, the sooner we start, the sooner we finish. Your parents haven't changed their number in the last few days, I take it?

CHARLOTTE looks at him warily as he picks up the phone and dials.

GEORGE: *(Into phone.)* Mr Chamberlain?... Oh I see... Yes, if you'd be so kind... No, he doesn't know me... *(Covers receiver.)* Well hark at me, imagining the Chamberlains would answer their own phones. I'm not even nouveau riche yet, and I've already made my first faux pas... *(Into phone.)* Mr Chamberlain?... It's about your daughter Charlotte... No, I realise she isn't there. She's here with me. That's what I wish to speak to you about, if you take my meaning... Well, you may call me George... That's right... Yes, that's precisely what I mean... Certainly Mr Chamberlain, just give me a moment to make the necessary arrangements. *(Covering phone, to CHARLOTTE.)* Miss Chamberlain, in a moment I'm going to remove your gag so that you can reassure your father that you're alive and well. But before I do that, I need you to understand two things. Firstly, this house is completely isolated. If you scream or cry out, no one other than Lennie and myself will hear you. Secondly, I guarantee that if you do as you're told, you will be treated well and no harm will come to you. However, cross me in any way and things can turn out very differently. I urge you most strongly not to put me to the test on this point. Nod your head to indicate that you understand.

After a moment CHARLOTTE nods.

GEORGE: Good. Now I want you to say to your father, 'Daddy'... Do you call him 'Daddy'?

She nods again.

GEORGE: Say to him 'Daddy, they're treating me well, but please give them what they want.' Nothing more, nothing less. Can you do that for me?

She nods again.

GEORGE: Good girl.

Putting the phone down on the table, GEORGE removes CHARLOTTE's gag. He holds the phone for her.

CHARLOTTE: *(Suddenly screaming in terror into the phone.)* Daddy please help me, please do whatever they want...

GEORGE snatches the phone away and covers the receiver again. CHARLOTTE fights to control her sobs.

GEORGE: *(Drily.)* A little more dramatic than I had in mind. Still, perhaps there's no harm in underlining the gravity of the situation. Lennie, would you mind?

LENNIE doesn't understand.

GEORGE: The gag.

LENNIE replaces her gag.

GEORGE: *(Into phone.)* Mr Chamberlain... *(Acidly.)* Oh, and I was so hoping we could be friends. Never mind, I shall just have to console myself with a large chunk of your money. Five million pounds, to be exact. You have precisely twenty-four hours to raise the money – though I suspect your daughter would be more than happy if you managed it sooner and we could all go home. She'll be released as soon as I have confirmation the money has been transferred... Oh come now, Mr Chamberlain, your flat in South Kensington is worth that by itself, your place in Berkshire at least three times as much... Yes, I know you can't sell a property overnight, that's not what I'm suggesting... Well, you have my demands, I suggest you start making the arrangements. I'll contact you again in a short while to give you the account details. In the meantime, let me just say that if you love your daughter you won't contact the police. I trust I don't need to make myself any clearer?… Until we speak again, Mr Chamberlain.

He puts the phone down.

LENNIE: *(Worried.)* He is gonna pay, isn't he? It sounded like he wasn't gonna pay.

GEORGE: Don't worry, he's just in shock. When he's had time to think it over, he'll see that paying up's his only option. Anyway, five million's just small change to people like him. *(Turning to CHARLOTTE.)* Well now, Miss Chamberlain, whatever shall we do with you? I realise the chloroform has probably left you with a bit of a headache, on top of which your plans for the evening changed suddenly at the last minute, and we all know how annoying that can be. But I think we'd all have a more pleasant evening if you didn't scream any more. As I told you, there really is no point. OK?

He walks across and removes her gag. She does not speak.

GEORGE: Well, I can't keep calling you Miss Chamberlain all night. So, Charlotte…though I understand you prefer Charlie?

CHARLOTTE looks daggers at him, a mixture of fear and contempt.

GEORGE: Please yourself. I was just trying to establish a congenial atmosphere, since fate has thrown us together like this.

CHARLOTTE: *(Incredulous.)* Fate?!?

GEORGE: *(Smiles.)* Well, I confess we might have helped fate along a little bit…

CHARLOTTE: *(Hysterical.)* You tied me up and locked me in the boot of my car!

GEORGE: Strictly speaking that was young Leonard here, though I do take your point. Nevertheless here we all are, and we may well be here for a while. I don't see any reason we can't be civilised about this.

CHARLOTTE: *(Scathingly.)* Civilised?

GEORGE: *(With an edge.)* Miss Chamberlain, you do have a way of looking at me as if I'm delivering the coal and I've forgotten to use the servants' entrance. But deep down, I think you know that the difference between you and me is an accident of birth, nothing more. If I'd been born into your family and had your advantages I'd be like you, and if you'd been born into mine you'd be like me, simple as that. We'd all know which knife to use if we had a butler to lay out the cutlery for us.

CHARLOTTE: *(Contemptuously.)* You think money is the only difference between us?

GEORGE: *(Acidly.)* Oh, don't tell me – you'd never stoop to doing something like this, is that it? Well maybe that's because you'd never have to. All you had to do to get rich is not fall off a pony until you were 18. So why don't you just be grateful for that, and do please forgive the rest of us if we have to make our own luck.

CHARLOTTE: Oh, is that what you're doing? Making your own luck?

GEORGE: You could say that.

CHARLOTTE: You really think this absurd scheme is going to make you rich?

GEORGE: Yes I do, and you'd better hope I'm right. I assure you the alternative is much worse for you than it is for me.

CHARLOTTE falls silent.

GEORGE: Still, no point getting ahead of ourselves. I'm sure your father will see sense and everything will turn out just fine.

CHARLOTTE: *(Nervously.)* He's telling you the truth. He can't come up with five million pounds, just like that.

GEORGE: *(Theatrically.)* Et tu, Bruté?

CHARLOTTE: I realise your idea of rich people comes entirely from airport novels, but you'll find they don't really keep their entire fortune in a wall safe behind a picture. My father may be wealthy, but his money's tied up in property, bonds, shares…

GEORGE: *(Breaking in.)* And like any wise investor, he made sure that a certain proportion of his investments could be realised immediately in case of sudden and unexpected need. This, I think you'll agree, is that moment. I didn't just blunder into this without doing my homework. At close of business yesterday, your father had in excess of five million pounds in investments of the kind I describe. Nearer six million, in fact, but let's not be greedy. If necessary, I can describe to him exactly how he can raise the money. But I'm sure it won't come to that. All the money in the world won't buy him another daughter.

CHARLOTTE: You've got it all figured out, haven't you?

GEORGE: Do you know, I rather think I have. *(Slight pause.)* Well, enough of this airy persiflage. Can I offer you some tea?

CHARLOTTE looks at him in astonishment.

CHARLOTTE: What?!?

GEORGE: Tea. You have heard of it, I suppose?

CHARLOTTE: *(Incredulously.)* You're offering to make me tea?

GEORGE: No staff here, I'm afraid. You know how it is – *(Snooty accent.)* 'the parlourmaid's run orf with the second footman and the hice is all at sixes and sevens.' *(She doesn't respond.)* Look, I'm making for me and Lennie, it's no extra effort to make one for you. Like I said, there's no reason we can't be civilised about this. I'm not some class warrior, out to take revenge on the rich – I just want to become one of them. *(Snooty accent again.)* 'And after all, we are British, don't you know, and we mustn't go letting standards slip just because we're in the middle of a horstage situation with simply lashings of money at stake…' *(Slight pause.)* Of course, if you're too grand to have tea with the likes of us…

CHARLOTTE: *(After a pause.)* Tea would be lovely, thank you.

GEORGE: And how does madame take it?

CHARLOTTE: *(Sarcastically.)* I'm amazed you don't know.

GEORGE: *(Laughs.)* I'm afraid my research wasn't quite that thorough.

CHARLOTTE: A little milk, no sugar.

GEORGE: Coming right up.

LENNIE: *(Guiltily.)* Oh, I never got no milk.

GEORGE: Well that was a bit thoughtless, wasn't it? You and I may not take it, but we do have our guest to consider. *(Drily.)* Or did you forget we were having company this evening?

LENNIE: Sorry. D'you want me to go and get some?

GEORGE: *(Sarcastically.)* From that convenience store across the road?

LENNIE: *(Surprised, turning to the window.)* Is there?

GEORGE: *(With infinite patience.)* No, Lennie.

LENNIE: There's a garage with a little shop a few miles down the road, by the roundabout. That's where I went before.

GEORGE: I saw it. *(A thought strikes him.)* It looked a bit basic. Did they have everything we need?

LENNIE: Well, they had tea and biscuits and that.

GEORGE: Is that all you got? Tea and biscuits?

LENNIE: And crisps. Oh, and some bread, in case you wanted a sandwich or toast or summink'.

GEORGE: Toast? What if we're here for days?

LENNIE: But you said he had to pay up in 24 hours!

GEORGE: That's what you might call an opening gambit, Lennie. We might have to compromise, give him a bit longer. Anyway, even if it is just 24 hours, what are we supposed to eat tonight?

LENNIE: *(Guiltily.)* I've already 'ad me tea.

GEORGE: *(Annoyed.)* Oh well that's alright then, isn't it? And what about the rest of us?

LENNIE: *(Ashamed.)* Sorry. I ain't done this before.

GEORGE: *(Irritably.)* What's that got to do with anything? None of us have. It's just simple common sense.

LENNIE: I just didn't wanna buy too much. Me mum always told me not to waste food.

GEORGE: I'm starting to think whatever your mum used to feed you was lacking in some vital nutrients. A bit more fish might have been a good idea, for a start.

Beat.

GEORGE: What kind of biscuits?

LENNIE: Hobnobs.

GEORGE: *(Hopefully.)* Chocolate ones?

LENNIE: No.

Clearly the wrong answer.

GEORGE: Well, tea and plain biscuits it is then.

He gets up and starts to head to the kitchen.

LENNIE: *(Remembers.)* Oh, I got some butter an' all. I put it in the fridge. But you might wanna take it out now so it'll be soft enough to spread later.

GEORGE: *(Drily.)* Thank you, Len. I'll come back to you if I need you to explain that in more detail. *(To CHARLOTTE.)* Sorry, I've forgotten already, did you want sugar?

CHARLOTTE: No.

GEORGE: You alright having it without milk?

CHARLOTTE: It's fine.

GEORGE: I'll just be a minute. Lennie here will look after you. *(With a smile.)* You mustn't mind if he stares at you. D'you know, I think he's taken rather a shine to you.

LENNIE, who was looking at CHARLOTTE, looks away quickly, embarrassed. GEORGE sets off towards the kitchen. At the doorway he pauses.

GEORGE: What kind of crisps?

LENNIE: Cheese and onion.

Wrong answer again. GEORGE exits to the kitchen. CHARLOTTE turns to LENNIE, who is still looking away, embarrassed by GEORGE's comment.

CHARLOTTE: *(Quietly, conspiratorially.)* Lennie…

LENNIE: *(Quickly.)* I wasn't lookin' at you.

CHARLOTTE: Never mind about that. Your name's Lennie, is that right?

LENNIE: *(After a pause.)* Might be.

CHARLOTTE: So tell me, Lennie. What's in this for you?

LENNIE: Me?

CHARLOTTE: I suppose he told you you'll get half the money when this is all over?

Beat.

LENNIE: *(Warily.)* What if he did?

CHARLOTTE: Come on Lennie, open your eyes. Did he even mention you during that big speech about making his own luck? He's thinking about no one but himself. Even if the plan comes off you'll never see a penny, and you'll almost certainly end up in prison. Do you really think he cares about you? He treats you like an idiot.

LENNIE: *(Stung.)* Tha's not true. He let me sort out this place, all by meself. He said I'd done really well.

CHARLOTTE: Oh he did, did he? So what, this place is rented, is it?

LENNIE looks uneasy, realising he has said too much.

CHARLOTTE: Yeah, that makes sense, he'd want your name to be on the rental agreement. And why do you think he got you to go to the local shop instead of doing it himself? Shops have security cameras, Lennie.

LENNIE: *(Starting to worry.)* No…he wouldn't do that…

CHARLOTTE: OK then, answer me this. If my father pays up, where's the money going? Which bank? What's the account number?

LENNIE: *(After a pause.)* I dunno. George sorted all that out.

CHARLOTTE: Well, there's a surprise. Come on Lennie, think about it. Anything involving risk, like kidnapping me, or renting this place, or being caught on camera, he gets you to do. Anything to do with the money, he completely cuts you out of. Can't you see what he's doing?

LENNIE: *(Mostly to reassure himself.)* He wouldn't do that…

CHARLOTTE: No, wait, you're right. He can't risk you being arrested, since you can identify him. He'll kill you, Lennie. As soon as he's got the money, he'll kill you.

LENNIE is stunned into silence. CHARLOTTE continues in a small, frightened voice.

CHARLOTTE: And now I've seen his face, he'll kill me too.

LENNIE: *(Looking in terror at the kitchen door.)* No…he wouldn't…

CHARLOTTE: *(Frightened.)* Of course he will. Think about it. What else can he do?

LENNIE: *(Confused, desperate.)* No, what it is, right…your dad's gonna pay up, and we're gonna be rich…

CHARLOTTE: *(Firmly.)* Forget about that, Lennie. That may have been the plan once, but things have changed. He'll kill me when he's got the money, he can't set me free now I've seen his face. And then he'll kill you.

Beat.

LENNIE: He said I shouldn't listen to nothin' you said.

CHARLOTTE: Well of course he bloody did, he wants you to go unsuspecting like a lamb to the slaughter.

LENNIE looks at the kitchen door in terror.

CHARLOTTE: *(Conspiratorially.)* Look, Lennie, you never meant to hurt me, I know that. And I'll make sure everyone else knows that too. I'll make sure you don't get in trouble. But you have to help me too, Lennie. We have to help each other. We can both get out of this alive if...

She falls silent instantly as GEORGE comes through the kitchen door carrying a tray with three mugs and a plate with a few slices of bread and jam.

GEORGE: Here we go. You don't mind mugs, I hope?

He sets the tray down on the table and passes two mugs to LENNIE, who looks worried.

GEORGE: Two sugars for you, and this one's for Miss Chamberlain. Maybe you'd better help her, Lennie.

GEORGE sits down in the armchair with his own tea. LENNIE puts his own mug down on the table, kneels down next to CHARLOTTE and holds up her mug so she can drink.

CHARLOTTE: It's a little hot just now, thank you Lennie. We'd better leave it a while.

LENNIE: Oh yeah, sorry.

GEORGE: I made some bread and jam too, just to keep us going. Would you care for some, Miss Chamberlain?

CHARLOTTE: *(With distaste.)* No thank you.

GEORGE: *(Helping himself.)* All the more for me. You didn't mention you'd bought jam, Lennie.

LENNIE: *(Bemused.)* I didn't. Must have been there already.

GEORGE, who has just bitten off a mouthful, stops chewing abruptly. Realising he has no alternative, he carries on chewing and swallows.

GEORGE: *(Uneasily.)* Seems alright anyway. I don't think it'd been opened. So...what shall we drink to?

Neither of them answer.

GEORGE: I know – to the future! No, hang on, isn't it bad luck to toast with anything non-alcoholic? Wouldn't want to jinx everything now we've come so far. *(He takes a sip of his tea.)* Mmm, yes, a little hot as you say. *(He puts the tea down.)* Well now, I'd say your father's had long enough to get over the shock, wouldn't you?

He picks up the telephone and dials.

GEORGE: *(Into phone.)* Hello, may I speak to… Ah, Mr Chamberlain… *(Covers mouthpiece.)* Answering the phone himself now, you notice… *(Into phone.)* The very same. I'm calling to give you the account details… *(With irritation.)* Mr Chamberlain, you disappoint me. You're insulting my intelligence and prolonging what must be a very unpleasant ordeal for your daughter. *(Covers mouthpiece, archly to LENNIE.)* She'll be sick to death of toast, apart from anything else. *(Into phone.)* As I was just telling her, the figure of five million wasn't plucked from thin air, it was chosen after detailed research into your financial affairs. In other words, I know for a fact that you can raise this amount, so there's really no point in you… Mr Chamberlain, I do hope you aren't making the mistake of thinking I'm not serious about this… Yes… I see… Mr Chamberlain, do you by any chance remember the Getty kidnapping a few years back? Remind me, what was it the kidnappers sent the father when he refused to pay the ransom? One of his son's fingers, wasn't it?

CHARLOTTE looks at LENNIE with alarm. LENNIE cannot meet her gaze.

GEORGE: *(Into phone.)* No, I tell a lie, it was an ear, wasn't it… Was it an ear? Hang on a second. *(Covers phone, to LENNIE.)* Lennie, d'you remember? Was it an ear?

LENNIE: *(Nervously.)* What?

GEORGE: The Getty kidnapping. When the father wouldn't pay the ransom, was it a finger they cut off and sent him, or an ear?

LENNIE: *(Bemused.)* Betty who?

GEORGE: Never mind. A bit before your time I suppose. *(Into phone.)* I'm afraid we're not quite sure at this end… Well it's the last thing I want to do, but if you persist in... If you would just stay calm I'm sure we could resolve matters to everyone's satisfaction... As I said before, contacting the police would be very unwise... I really don't think there's any call for that kind of language... Mr Chamberlain, I'll call you back later when you've calmed down...goodbye, Mr Chamberlain.

He puts the phone down.

GEORGE: *(To CHARLOTTE.)* He really has quite a temper, doesn't he? Is he like that at home? You know, there's probably some sort of helpline you could call...

CHARLOTTE: *(Explodes.)* You bloody psychopath!

GEORGE: *(Ironically.)* Well, it seems the apple didn't fall far from the tree...

CHARLOTTE: *(Cold fury.)* You're making a big mistake. My father is not someone you want as an enemy.

LENNIE: *(Crossing the room to GEORGE, conspiratorially.)* George?

GEORGE: Yes, Len?

LENNIE: You never said nothin' about this.

GEORGE: About what?

LENNIE: You know, about...what you said. About her fingers an' ears an' that.

GEORGE: Oh, that. Don't worry, that was just for his benefit.

LENNIE: *(Puzzled.)* His...benefit?

GEORGE: I just want him to think we'll do it if he doesn't pay up.

LENNIE: *(Relieved.)* Oh...so we're not really gonna do it?

GEORGE: *(After a pause.)* I suppose I'm saying that threatening to do it is probably as far as we'll need to go. You understand?

LENNIE: I think so. And when we've got the money, we let her go, yeah?

GEORGE: *(Seemingly surprised.)* Of course, Lennie. What do you take me for? Trust me, I've got this all worked out. *(He looks at his watch.)* Well, *(Pointedly.)* those of us who *haven't* eaten are starting to feel a bit peckish now.

LENNIE: I can go back to that garage, see if they…

He tails off as he remembers the security cameras.

GEORGE: They'll be closed by now anyway. Don't worry, toast'll do for tonight. We can have a rethink in the morning if needs be.

He goes into the kitchen, taking the tray with him. LENNIE does not look at CHARLOTTE.

CHARLOTTE: *(Urgent whisper.)* Lennie!

LENNIE: *(Still not looking at her.)* What?

CHARLOTTE: You've got to do something!

LENNIE: Me?

CHARLOTTE: I saw your reaction just now. You know this is wrong. You've got to do something now before things go too far.

LENNIE: No, he ain't really gonna do it. It was just pretend. He explained it all to me.

CHARLOTTE: No, Lennie, that's not what he said at all.

LENNIE: But he said…

CHARLOTTE: Lennie, listen to me. This is your last chance to stop this. You've got to do something now, before he comes back, or you'll end up dead or in prison for life. If you help me get away, I promise I'll make sure that doesn't happen.

LENNIE: *(Looks nervously at kitchen door.)* I can't. He'd be mad at me.

CHARLOTTE: *(Exasperated.)* Mad at you? For God's sake Lennie, this is your life we're talking about. And mine. What's more important?

LENNIE doesn't move.

CHARLOTTE: Alright, Lennie, how about this. He doesn't have to know you helped me. Just loosen the cord around my wrists. You can say I got free by myself and took off before you could do anything about it. He'll never know you had anything to do with it. OK?

LENNIE looks between her and the kitchen door in an agony of indecision.

CHARLOTTE: Come on Lennie, there's no time. You know this is wrong. You're a good man, Lennie, I know you are. That's why he won't tell you the truth about what he's going to do. This is your last chance to stop this and save both our lives.

Suddenly LENNIE rushes over to her and starts to undo the cord around her wrists.

GEORGE: *(Calling from the kitchen.)* I suppose you did actually check there was a toaster?

LENNIE looks at the kitchen door in panic.

LENNIE: *(Calling.)* Er, it might be in one of the cupboards.

GEORGE: *(Off.)* I've looked there.

LENNIE: *(Desperately.)* Well, we can have sandwiches then.

LENNIE turns back to find that CHARLOTTE has her hands free and has now started to untie her feet. He is frozen in panic for a moment.

LENNIE: *(Panicked.)* Sorry, I can't do it. He'd never believe me.

He struggles with her, trying to get her tied up again.

GEORGE: *(Off.)* And what are we supposed to have in the sandwiches? Thin air?

LENNIE: *(Calling, trying to keep the panic out of his voice.)* I got some cheese. It's in the fridge.

GEORGE: *(Off.)* What kind?

LENNIE: *(Calling.)* Y'know. Ordinary.

GEORGE: *(Off.)* Cheddar, you mean? *(Pause.)* It's not sliced. What am I supposed to slice it with?

Suddenly CHARLOTTE grabs hold of LENNIE's gun from his waistband and points it at him.

CHARLOTTE: *(With quiet menace.)* Back off, Lennie. I mean it. I don't want to hurt you, but I'm not staying here so that bloody lunatic can post me home in weekly installments.

LENNIE backs off in terror, while CHARLOTTE finishes untying her feet. LENNIE looks in panic between her and the kitchen door.

LENNIE: *(Shouting in panic.)* Mr Re... George! It's not my fault...

CHARLOTTE: *(Hissing urgently.)* Be quiet, Lennie!

LENNIE: She's got loose... George!

CHARLOTTE: *(Urgently.)* Shut up! My car keys, where are they?

LENNIE produces her car keys from his pocket.

CHARLOTTE: Put them on the table.

He does.

CHARLOTTE: Now back away.

LENNIE backs away. CHARLOTTE keeps him covered with the gun while trying to retrieve her keys, but she has to take her eyes off him while picking them up and he takes the opportunity to rush her. They struggle again, the gun between them, and a shot rings out. LENNIE collapses slowly to the floor, never taking his eyes off CHARLOTTE. A bloodstain starts spreading on his shirt. Horrified by what she has done, she stands rooted to the spot.

GEORGE walks in casually from the kitchen, eating a bag of crisps. CHARLOTTE immediately swings the gun to point at him.

GEORGE: *(Calmly.)* D'you know, I didn't think I liked cheese and onion. But they're actually not that bad.

CHARLOTTE: Stay where you are!

Seemingly oblivious to her, he walks across the room towards LENNIE's body, still eating the crisps. She tracks him with the gun all the way. He crouches by LENNIE's body for a moment, then stands up again.

GEORGE: Very good shot, Miss Chamberlain. But then, I guess he was a pretty easy target compared to a grouse.

CHARLOTTE: *(With menace.)* Back off. I'd have no compunction about killing you too.

GEORGE: Oh, I'm sure you'd be more than happy to. But I think you'll find there was only one bullet in that gun, and you've just used it.

She doesn't move.

GEORGE: Check, if you don't believe me. You do know how to open a gun, I suppose? Or do the beaters do all that for you?

CHARLOTTE: So you can overpower me while I'm defenceless? I don't think so.

GEORGE: Dear me, such a suspicious mind. Tell you what, I'll stand over here and face the wall if that makes you feel safer.

He walks to the far end of the room facing the wall. She tracks him all the way with the gun.

CHARLOTTE: Maybe I'll check by pulling the trigger again.

GEORGE: *(Calmly.)* Feel free.

Beat.

CHARLOTTE: Loaders.

GEORGE: Beg pardon?

CHARLOTTE: Not beaters. The loaders look after the guns. The beaters drive the grouse out of the undergrowth.

GEORGE: Well, thanks for putting me straight on that. I'd hate to make a fool of myself come the glorious twelfth.

CHARLOTTE opens the gun and confirms to her horror that there are no more bullets.

GEORGE: Mind if I turn round now?

He does. He is now holding a gun pointing directly at her.

GEORGE: This one, on the other hand, is fully loaded. Put the gun on the table, please. Nice and slowly. We don't want any more accidents.

She does.

GEORGE: If you wouldn't mind passing me those cords? I don't think we'll be needing them any more, unless the evening takes a very unexpected turn.

She does. He puts them in his coat pocket.

GEORGE: Do sit down.

CHARLOTTE: *(Indicates the sofa.)* Here?

GEORGE: Sounds favourite. Your tea should be cool enough to drink by now. Finish Lennie's too if you want, though you might find it a tad sweet. I was always telling him so much sugar was bad for him, but would he listen?

She sits on the sofa, he in the armchair. He produces a handkerchief from his pocket and uses it to pick up the gun without touching it.

GEORGE: Good old mum, always told me never to leave the house without a clean hankie. *(Drily.)* Though frankly I can't imagine she foresaw this situation.

He puts the bundle in his coat pocket.

GEORGE: I do hope Lennie wasn't too rough with you, by the way, in the car park. His heart was in the right place – *(Smiles.)* well, you certainly proved that – but there's no denying he was a bit of a blunt instrument. It seems all those years at finishing school just didn't do the trick. Or perhaps they just let him out too early, before he was finished. Who knows. Still, he won't be bothering anyone else now, will he? You've made sure of that.

CHARLOTTE: *(Anguished.)* I had no choice. It was my only chance of getting away.

GEORGE: And yet here you still are. It seems poor Lennie died for nothing. What a pity.

CHARLOTTE: *(Acidly.)* Oh, I'm sure you're just heartbroken. As if he would have lived much longer anyway.

GEORGE: *(Innocently.)* Whatever do you mean?

CHARLOTTE: Lennie might not have figured you out, but I have. You weren't going to share the ransom with him. You were setting him up to take the blame while you got away with all the money.

GEORGE: *(With mock innocence.)* Me?

CHARLOTTE: Why else would you make sure this place was rented in his name? And that he was the one caught on camera in the local shop?

Beat. GEORGE looks at her.

GEORGE: And in your garage, of course.

CHARLOTTE: What?

GEORGE: Security cameras. Though none anywhere near your parking space, as it happens. You really should take that up with the management, by the way. I hate to think how much service charge you're paying, and frankly it seems to me they're being rather cavalier about your safety. Anyway, there's a camera by the entrance, so that'll have caught him.

CHARLOTTE: I knew it. I knew you were setting him up.

GEORGE: Yes, honour among thieves is purely a myth, I'm afraid. Just one of those things people stubbornly insist on believing in, like the tooth fairy, leprechauns or taxis south of the river. But what makes you think he didn't have long to live?

CHARLOTTE: Well, it's obvious isn't it? He could identify you, there's no way you were going to leave him alive. You were going to leave a trail of evidence leading straight to him, and then make sure he couldn't tell anyone the truth.

GEORGE: Well, aren't you a clever girl? *(Slight pause.)* So clever, in fact, that I'm sure something else must have occurred to you.

CHARLOTTE: What?

GEORGE: Well, I hate to bring up such a delicate subject, but you can identify me too.

Beat. CHARLOTTE says nothing.

GEORGE: And all because you pulled off Lennie's balaclava. Not such a good idea as it seemed at the time, eh?

CHARLOTTE: *(Fearfully.)* Look, there's no way my father will pay you a penny until he knows I've been released, safe and well.

GEORGE: Well, you say that, but I told him you'd be released *after* I had confirmation that the money had been transferred, and he seemed perfectly happy with that. After all, if I let you go first, he's got no reason to pay me anything at all.

CHARLOTTE says nothing.

GEORGE: Oh, don't give up hope Miss Chamberlain, maybe you can talk me out of it. It worked a treat on Lennie, after all. *(Sarcastically imitating her sympathetic tone.)* 'I'll protect you... I'll make sure you don't go to prison...'

CHARLOTTE: *(Astonished.)* You could hear?

GEORGE: *(Smiling.)* The serving hatch was open. Frankly I'm surprised you weren't more alert to the danger. Must be the bane of your life, the upstairs maid overhearing your private conversations, gossiping with the under-butler in the downstairs pantry... By the way, is it true you never look directly at a servant? I've always wondered.

Beat.

GEORGE: I only ask because I was surprised you didn't recognise Lennie.

CHARLOTTE: *(Taken aback.)* Recognise him?

GEORGE: That's right, princess. Implausible as it may seem, you have had the pleasure of meeting our Lennie before.

She looks at the body again with a shudder.

GEORGE: Ah, but where can it have been, she wonders. On the dance floor at Boujis? On the slopes at Gstaad? On a yacht off the Riviera? *(Slight pause.)* You've really no idea?

She shakes her head.

GEORGE: Clever old Lennie, he said you wouldn't remember him. The rather mundane truth is that he occasionally worked as a waiter for a catering company. Last summer they did the food for what was by all accounts a rather swanky affair in Holland Park. He told me he poured you several glasses of champagne in the course of the evening – though I don't suppose that narrows it down too much for you. That was when you first came to our attention. Of course, he wasn't calling himself Lennie then. I suppose you realised that wasn't his real name?

CHARLOTTE: *(Sarcastically.)* No kidding. George and Lennie? I did it for A-level.

GEORGE: Good to see Steinbeck's penetrated as far as Roedean. *(Amused.)* It was a little unkind of me, I suppose. But then, he didn't understand the reference, so where's the harm? Anyway, his real name doesn't matter. Not when he was alive, and certainly not now. But you might know him best as Old Acquaintance. His nom de plume, if you like.

Beat.

CHARLOTTE: *(Taken aback.)* Old Acquaintance?

GEORGE: That's right.

Beat.

CHARLOTTE: You mean…

GEORGE: Yes, Miss Chamberlain?

Beat.

CHARLOTTE: Those emails…were from him?

GEORGE: Got it in one.

CHARLOTTE is stunned, taking it all in.

CHARLOTTE: I thought it must be some kid messing about.

GEORGE: Yes, I'm afraid the late unlamented Leonard wasn't the most articulate of men. I told him basically what to say, of course, but I had to leave him to put it in his own words. Internet cafes tend to have security cameras too, and naturally I couldn't have the footage showing me as well. So I can imagine his emails weren't exactly Tolstoy.

CHARLOTTE: They didn't make any sense at all. Just kept going on about some guilty secret from my past that he'd go public with unless I paid him off.

GEORGE: I gather you didn't take his threats seriously?

CHARLOTTE: Of course not, he couldn't even spell my name. Or 'acquaintance'. Anyway, it was obvious he was bluffing. If he'd really had anything to blackmail me with, he would have said what it was.

GEORGE: Do you know, he raised exactly the same objection to me. 'What is this big secret? What's she done?' I told him he didn't need to know. All he had to do was convince you he knew something, and you'd get frightened and pay up.

CHARLOTTE: *(Scornfully.)* I see. And when this pathetic attempt at blackmail failed, you thought you'd kidnap me instead.

GEORGE: *(With mock innocence.)* Kidnap, Miss Chamberlain? Whatever do you mean?

CHARLOTTE: *(Incredulous.)* What do I mean?!? You're sitting there pointing a gun at me.

GEORGE: Hardly an unreasonable precaution in the circumstances. You've already killed one man tonight. Still, perhaps you're right – now that you're safely disarmed, I can afford to relax a little.

He puts his gun in his pocket.

CHARLOTTE: What the hell are you talking about?

GEORGE: Why Miss Chamberlain, I'm talking about your motive in coming here tonight.

CHARLOTTE: *(Incredulous.)* My *motive?*

GEORGE: I think it's pretty clear what happened. You receive a series of emails demanding money with menaces. The last email, sent at noon today, tells you to bring the money to this address at nine o'clock tonight. *(Checks watch.)* That's about what time it is now, isn't it?

CHARLOTTE: *(Surprised.)* I haven't seen that email.

GEORGE: Oh, that's right, you've been out all day, haven't you? Well, I'm sure you'll have no problem in court as long as you explain that.

CHARLOTTE: *(Taken aback.)* In court?

During the following, CHARLOTTE becomes more and more visibly alarmed.

GEORGE: The security footage in your garage will show your car arriving home at about six this evening and leaving again 20 minutes later. Now, what were you doing for that 20 minutes, I wonder? Perhaps you went up to your flat, checked your email and saw to your dismay that there was yet another threatening message from this mysterious 'Old Acquaintance'. But this time he's made a fatal mistake. He's told you where you can find him. So you set off again, pausing only to grab the gun you keep in your bedside drawer in case of emergencies. After all, if this isn't an emergency, what is? You can't risk this terrible secret coming out, and desperate times call for desperate measures.

And now the blackmailer's lying dead at that same address, killed by a bullet fired from a gun with only your fingerprints on it. They can match bullets to the gun that fired them, did you know that? Terribly clever, those forensics boffins. *(Breezily.)* But what am I saying? As you said, you never saw the email, so everything else is…just a coincidence. *(As a pompous barrister.)* 'That concludes the case for the defence, m'lord.'

CHARLOTTE: *(Agitated.)* But... I didn't come here voluntarily! I wasn't driving the car, I was tied up and locked in the boot!

GEORGE: Hmm. Trouble is, as I mentioned, there's no camera covering your parking space. You really should complain about that, you know. So why should anyone doubt that you were driving the car when it left again?

CHARLOTTE: *(Desperately.)* But...he kidnapped me and brought me here! I don't even know where this place is! And the gun isn't mine, I've never seen it before.

GEORGE: Well, you say that, but it only has your fingerprints on it. And what's all this talk of kidnapping? That really is a very serious allegation. I do hope you have some evidence to back it up?

CHARLOTTE: *(Exasperated.)* Evidence?!? Well of course I... *(An idea strikes her.)* The phone calls to my father! What about them?

GEORGE: Ah, I must confess I told you a little white lie there. Those phone calls were to my own answering machine. Oh, thanks for reminding me – I must delete those messages when I get home. *(Smiles.)* Though I confess I might listen to them once or twice first. Savour the moment, as it were.

CHARLOTTE sits in stunned silence, taking it all in. She looks again at LENNIE's body.

GEORGE: Oh don't look so downcast, Miss Chamberlain, it's not all bad news. The fact is, the police aren't likely to bust a gut looking for Lennie's killer. When he wasn't serving the amusing New Zealand chardonnay, our Lennie was what you might call an errand boy for an East-End firm. That means an organised crime syndicate, by the way, in case you were imagining a firm of accountants.

CHARLOTTE: *(Irritably.)* I know what it means.

GEORGE: Then you'll appreciate it's not exactly the healthiest of professions to be in. Maybe he was killed in a turf war with another gang. Maybe his employers thought he was skimming a bit off the top for himself, or maybe they found out he was moonlighting and took a dim view of it. There must be a dozen possibilities. The police won't even bother to yawn. And they won't in their wildest dreams imagine some trust fund babe from South Ken had anything to do with it.

CHARLOTTE does not respond.

GEORGE: Then again, if they were to get hold of the gun that killed him and find your fingerprints all over it… *(He takes out the camera, finds the photo and shows it to her.)* Or for that matter this photo of your car arriving here. Isn't it clever how these digital cameras record not only the time a photo was taken, but also the location? Geotagging, it's called. Something to do with satellites apparently. *(With mock disappointment.)* Oh, how careless of me, the way I've taken it you can't see who's driving the car. Never mind, the number plate's nice and clear. The police will assume Lennie took it as you arrived, as an insurance policy in case anything went wrong. *(He turns off the camera and replaces it in his pocket.)* So you see, Miss Chamberlain, you were quite right that I was leaving a trail of evidence. You just didn't realise who it was leading to.

Well, this new evidence leaves the police very confused. Why would high society party girl Charlotte Chamberlain drive to the middle of nowhere to shoot some no account lowlife? So they dig a little deeper. They find the emails he sent you. And they begin to piece it all together. Petty criminal, mixing with the upper classes while working as a waiter, stumbles onto something he can use to blackmail wealthy socialite. He tells her to bring the money to an isolated spot where they won't be observed. But she, knowing she'll never be safe while this unscrupulous thug knows her terrible secret, decides there's only one way to get him out of her life permanently.

CHARLOTTE: *(Exasperated.)* What secret? I don't have any bloody secret!

GEORGE: Who knows? Maybe you didn't. *(Glancing at LENNIE's body.)* But I'd have to say, Miss Chamberlain, you do now.

Beat.

GEORGE: As to whether or not the police ever get that new evidence…that depends on you.

Beat.

CHARLOTTE: *(With quiet dread.)* So what is it you want?

GEORGE: What I want, Miss Chamberlain, is money. Truckloads of it.

Beat.

CHARLOTTE: I honestly don't have that much.

GEORGE: *(Drily.)* Oh yes? I wonder if your idea of not much is the same as mine…

CHARLOTTE: Look, I know what kind of life you think I lead. All that crap about Gstaad and yachts on the Riviera. But the truth is I get an allowance, that's all. A trust fund. And yes, it does give me a pretty good lifestyle, I'm not denying that. But if you think I've got millions just sitting in the bank, you're barking up the wrong tree.

GEORGE: I'm well aware of that, Miss Chamberlain. I told you, I didn't just stumble into this without doing my research. You may not have a fortune in the bank, but you'll be happy to know you have something even more valuable, at least to me.

CHARLOTTE: And what's that?

GEORGE: You're a director of your father's company, Chamberlain Industries, are you not?

CHARLOTTE: *(Surprised.)* Well…technically I am, yes.

GEORGE: Oh, I realise you don't actually do anything for the money. But you know what? I think all that's about to change. You're 25 now, I believe?

CHARLOTTE: *(Uncertainly.)* Ye-es.

GEORGE: Just the sort of age where you might feel you want to settle down and do something meaningful with your life. And to daddy's inexpressible joy, you decide to go into the family business. So you immerse yourself in learning how it all works, what pays for all the fast cars and polo ponies. And one day your eye is caught by something the research and development people are working on. It's all very hush hush, but that only arouses your curiosity even more. Just what is this mysterious Omega project?

CHARLOTTE: Omega project?

GEORGE: You see how hush hush it is? Even the company directors don't know about it. *(Drily.)* Or just sign things without bothering to read them, perhaps. But the fact is they have very good reason to keep it under wraps. You see, in a nutshell, Omega is a breakthrough in the development of semiconductors which should, barring accidents, make Chamberlain Industries a very large amount of money indeed and put them ahead of their competitors for a generation. So naturally, at this stage they have to keep it quiet.

CHARLOTTE: So how the hell do you know about it?

GEORGE: Well now, that's an interesting question. And to be quite honest, even I don't know the first few links in the chain. But however it happened, your father's competitors got wind of what he was up to. Only a vague idea, but enough for them to know that he stood to make an almost inconceivable amount of money. But – and this part's crucial, so pay attention – they also knew that he hadn't yet secured the patent. A few minor glitches still to be ironed out. So they thought to themselves, if we could get hold of the full technical specs, we could put our best people on it, work around the clock and get the patent for ourselves. Then when your father turns up at the patent office, the plans clutched in his sweaty little hands, he's out of luck. Someone else has beaten him to it.

CHARLOTTE: They'd never believe that. Two separate companies coming up with the same invention at the same time?

GEORGE: Even if they don't, who's stealing from whom? The fact remains that your father's competitors got there first, and their prior claim has to be honoured.

But of course, for this to work they have to get hold of the plans to Omega as soon as possible. And that urgency, I'm happy to say, means they're prepared to pay really rather a lot for them. Ten million pounds, to be exact.

Which, of course, is where I come into the story. And now you.

Beat.

CHARLOTTE: Oh no. You can't be serious.

GEORGE: I never joke about money, Miss Chamberlain. At least, not about that much money.

CHARLOTTE: You expect me to get you the plans? Betray my own father for money?

GEORGE: *(Apparently shocked.)* Of course not, Miss Chamberlain, I wouldn't dream of asking such a thing of you. *(Slight pause.)* No, the money's all for me. What you get in return is that the police never get hold of the evidence linking you to laughing boy over there.

CHARLOTTE: *(Anguished.)* My own father…

GEORGE: Your loyalty is very touching, but when you consider that the alternative would somewhat mess up your plans for the rest of your life, I suspect you'll come round to my way of thinking.

CHARLOTTE says nothing.

GEORGE: Look, Chamberlain's a highly profitable company, it's not as if Omega is the only thing standing between him and bankruptcy. You'll carry on living exactly as you do now, exactly *where* you do now, and so will he. And he'll never know it was you who betrayed him.

CHARLOTTE: That's not the point!

GEORGE: Isn't it? Well, I don't pretend to be a moral philosopher. If you'd rather spend twenty years in prison for murder, go right ahead. Though it does seem a terrible shame. A young woman in your position, with so much to look forward to…

CHARLOTTE: *(Horrified.)* Twenty years…

GEORGE: 'Fraid so. Premeditation, you see – bringing the gun, coming here with the intention of killing him. Makes it murder rather than manslaughter.

CHARLOTTE says nothing.

GEORGE: Still, maybe it won't be so bad. You went to boarding school, after all – how different can it be? Not quite so much lacrosse, perhaps, but I'm told you get half an hour's exercise in the yard every day. And, er – *(Smiles.)* also like boarding school, or so I'm told – you don't have to go without in other areas either. Of course, I can't promise your cellmate will be quite so glamorous, but then again, you might not look so good yourself after a few years…

CHARLOTTE: *(Irritably.)* All right, all right. You've made your point.

GEORGE: So we have an understanding?

Beat. CHARLOTTE looks at him.

CHARLOTTE: *(Quietly.)* Yes.

GEORGE: *(Smiles.)* That's my girl.

GEORGE rises.

GEORGE: Well, a profitable and, if I may say, an enjoyable evening, but it's time we were making a move. They generally can't determine the time of death too precisely, but we'd better not push our luck. Time to call the police now.

CHARLOTTE: *(Alarmed.)* The police?

GEORGE: Of course. Did you think I was just going to leave him for the cleaner to find his decomposing carcass in a week's time? That just wouldn't be nice.

He picks up the phone.

GEORGE: But don't worry, it'll take them at least fifteen minutes to trace the call and get someone out here. That gives us plenty of time to get away. Oh, hang on a second.

He picks up CHARLOTTE's car keys from the table and tosses to them her.

GEORGE: Your car keys, madam.

She catches them. He picks up his and her mugs, leaving just LENNIE's on the table.

GEORGE: You'd better follow me until we get back to London and you know where you are. After that, of course, we'll be heading in different directions. *(Smiles.)* Though I do hope to be moving to a much better part of town very soon. We might even be neighbours! Now wouldn't that be cosy?

Hang on, you'd better let me open the door so you don't leave any prints.

He opens the front door for her.

GEORGE: Well, tempus fugit, Miss Chamberlain. Time's wingèd chariot, and all that. If you don't get me the plans before your father gets his patent, I don't get paid, and that scenario doesn't end well for you.

In the meantime, you'd better get home to your family. *(Smiles.)* After all, we wouldn't want them to worry that something had happened to you.

He dials 999.

GEORGE: *(Into phone.)* Police.

He sets the receiver down on the floor by LENNIE's outstretched hand. She goes to speak but he silences her with a finger to his lips, indicating the telephone. She goes through the front door. He is about to follow when he looks back at the room, sees the plate of bread and jam and darts back to grab just one more slice. He then follows her through the door, turning off the light and closing the door behind him, leaving complete darkness.

End of Act One.

Act Two

The same setting, this time in daylight. A car is heard approaching as GEORGE emerges from the kitchen, mug of tea in hand. The car door opens and closes. Footsteps, then the back (kitchen) door is tried but won't open. More footsteps, then a ring at the front doorbell. GEORGE answers the door to CHARLOTTE. She is wearing high heels and carrying a large handbag.

GEORGE: Miss Chamberlain, how very lovely to see you again.

CHARLOTTE walks past GEORGE without a word.

GEORGE: *(Drily.)* Won't you come in?

CHARLOTTE: The back door was locked.

GEORGE: I know, I couldn't find the key.

CHARLOTTE: *(With venom.)* I really can't believe you'd make me come here again.

GEORGE: *(Innocently.)* You were the one who wanted to meet up.

CHARLOTTE: But not here, for God's sake! Do you get some sort of sadistic pleasure from putting me through this?

GEORGE: *(As if mortally offended.)* Miss Chamberlain, it grieves me that you could think such a thing of me, truly it does. As it happens, I have to be here later. Since you insist on seeing me this morning, it has to be here. If you could wait until tomorrow…

CHARLOTTE: *(Interrupting.)* It can't wait!

GEORGE: Well, there you are then. Your decision. Can I offer you a drink of some kind? Well, having said that, there's only tea. Still no milk, of course…

CHARLOTTE: *(Impatiently.)* Bugger the bloody tea.

GEORGE: All right then. So what did you want to see me about?

She sits down on the sofa.

CHARLOTTE: He knows!

GEORGE: *(Solemnly.)* Right. I see. *(Slight pause.)* Who knows what?

CHARLOTTE: My father! He knows the Omega plans have been leaked.

GEORGE: *(With mock horror.)* Surely not!

CHARLOTTE: I've never seen him so furious. He kept ranting and raving about what he was going to do when he found out who was responsible. I just can't understand it. I covered my tracks every step of the way. How the hell did he find out?

GEORGE sits in the chair and ponders.

GEORGE: *(Pensively.)* Hmm… You know, now that I think about it, there's only one way he could have found out.

CHARLOTTE: *(Surprised.)* How?

GEORGE: I told him.

CHARLOTTE: *(Aghast.)* You did what?

GEORGE: *(Calmly.)* I told him I was in possession of a copy of the plans of the Omega project.

CHARLOTTE: *(Explodes.)* What the hell did you do that for?

GEORGE: I just wanted to give the old boy a fair chance. I told him I had the plans, and one of his competitors was willing to pay me ten million for them. A tempting offer, of course, but if he were to pay me twice that amount, the plans would stay safely locked away. And I'm pleased to say he was admirably level-headed about it. Then again, he stands to make hundreds of millions if he can get the patent, so why wouldn't he pay twenty million now to make hundreds later? It's simple common sense. Come to think of it, I should probably have asked for more…

CHARLOTTE: You devious bastard.

GEORGE: Miss Chamberlain, you really must learn not to take these things so personally. It's just business.

CHARLOTTE takes a deep breath.

CHARLOTTE: *(With determination.)* That's why I'm here. To talk business.

GEORGE: *(Surprised.)* Oh yes?

CHARLOTTE: I want my share.

Beat.

GEORGE: Excuse me?

CHARLOTTE: 50%. That's what you were going to give Lennie, or so you told him anyway. Well, he's no longer a factor. I'm your new partner.

GEORGE: *(Amused.)* I see. And…er…do I get any say in this?

CHARLOTTE: *(With steely determination.)* Look, I'm the one who was put through hell that night. Snatched from my own home, chloroformed, tied up, locked in the boot of my car and taken to the middle of nowhere. I really thought I wouldn't get out of here alive. And I'm the one who… *(She tails off, glancing at the place on the floor where LENNIE's body fell.)*

GEORGE: Ah yes. Poor Lennie.

CHARLOTTE: *(Vitriolically.)* Oh, as if you ever gave a crap about him. I killed him because I thought it was the only way to save my own life. *(Slight pause.)* And I'll always have to live with that. You sacrificed him in cold blood, and for no better reason than money.

GEORGE: Oh, do come down from the stained glass window, dear. You might not think money so beneath you if you hadn't been born rolling in it.

CHARLOTTE: *(Angrily.)* I've told you, I…

Beat.

CHARLOTTE: *(More in control.)* Anyway, what's done is done. What matters is where we go from here. And I think you owe me.

GEORGE: *Owe* you?

CHARLOTTE: For what I went through that night. Without me there wouldn't be any money to discuss.

GEORGE: You were a somewhat unwilling participant in the proceedings, if memory serves...

CHARLOTTE: Nevertheless, the fact remains you only have that money because of me. Anyway, if you've now got twenty million, giving me half will still leave you ten.

GEORGE: *(Sarcastically.)* Oh, well that's alright then, isn't it? But, er, unless I'm being very slow on the uptake, I don't see why I should give you anything at all. Or were you just relying on me being *(Snooty accent.)* 'a thoroughly decent chap who plays the game with a straight bat'?

CHARLOTTE: *(Contemptuously.)* Hardly.

GEORGE: Well, what then?

Beat.

CHARLOTTE: You give me half the money, or my father finds out.

Beat.

GEORGE: Finds out what?

CHARLOTTE: Everything.

Beat.

GEORGE: Is that right?

CHARLOTTE: Yep. I'll tell him all about you kidnapping and blackmailing me. Oh, and now it seems you've been extorting money out of him too. I assume in these negotiations with him, you didn't use your real name?

GEORGE says nothing.

CHARLOTTE: I thought not. You kept it anonymous, opened a bank account in a false name for him to pay the money into. Was that it?

Beat.

GEORGE: Something like that.

CHARLOTTE: Very wise. Well, if you want to stay anonymous it'll cost you half the money. And I'm not talking about the police. My father has his own people, and his own methods.

GEORGE: I see. And when he asks how I came to have the Omega plans in the first place, what then?

CHARLOTTE: *(Simply.)* I'll tell him the truth. He won't blame me when he knows I was being blackmailed. In fact, it'll just make him all the more furious with you.

GEORGE: And if he asks what you were being blackmailed about? Will you tell him that as well?

Beat.

GEORGE: Then again, I suppose you wouldn't have to. He could just read about it in the papers.

CHARLOTTE: *(Alarmed.)* What?

GEORGE: You seem to be forgetting that I have the evidence against you in safe keeping. Believe me, I know full well who your father is and what he's capable of. So I took out a little insurance policy. If anything untoward happens to me – no matter how innocent or accidental it may seem – my solicitor has instructions to retrieve the gun and the camera and give them to the police.

Beat.

GEORGE: So you see, Miss Chamberlain, you can ruin me, but I can ruin you too.

CHARLOTTE: I killed him in self defence. No jury in the world would convict me.

GEORGE: *(As a pompous barrister.)* 'Ah yes, this far-fetched kidnap story of yours. Highly entertaining, Miss

Chamberlain. But do you really expect this court to believe it, in the face of the evidence that the man you killed was blackmailing you?'

CHARLOTTE: Even if they don't, all you can do is put me in prison. I can get you killed.

GEORGE: Perhaps, but I can't see you doing it. I don't think knowing I was dead would be much comfort to you during the long years inside.

CHARLOTTE: *(With feeling.)* Oh, it might.

GEORGE: And then there's daddy to consider. You really think he'll just forgive and forget if he finds out how you've betrayed him? To say nothing of the scandal of his daughter going to prison. I bet he's quite sensitive about that kind of thing, isn't he? The ones who made their own money are always that bit more insecure. So I don't imagine he'd be a frequent visitor at Holloway. And you can certainly forget about any inheritance you were counting on. Is it really worth giving up all that just to see me dead?

CHARLOTTE says nothing.

GEORGE: I mean, seriously, you earning your own living? Do you actually know how to do anything? *(Smiles.)* Still, maybe they'll teach you a trade inside – woodwork, laundry, basket-weaving…

CHARLOTTE: *(Defeated.)* All right, all right.

GEORGE: So I'm afraid I must respectfully decline your offer of partnership. *(Slight pause.)* Are you sure you won't have any tea?

CHARLOTTE: *(Steely determination.)* This isn't the end of it, George. Not by a long w…

She stops in her tracks, hearing the sound of another car approaching. During the following we hear it park, the engine stop, the door open and close and footsteps up to the door.

GEORGE: That must be Inspector Crichton. *(Checks watch.)* He's a bit early, isn't he?

CHARLOTTE: *(Alarmed.)* Inspector? The police?

GEORGE: That's right.

CHARLOTTE: What's he doing here?

GEORGE: He called me, said he wanted to speak to me.

CHARLOTTE: What about?

GEORGE: No idea. He just gave me this address and told me to meet him here.

CHARLOTTE: *(Terrified.)* Oh my God, he mustn't see me here with you. Is there another way out?

GEORGE: Only the back door.

CHARLOTTE starts towards the kitchen, then remembers.

CHARLOTTE: It's locked!

GEORGE: I know, I told you I couldn't find the key. You'll just have to hide in the kitchen until he's gone. And for God's sake keep quiet.

There is a knock at the front door. CHARLOTTE grabs her bag and rushes into the kitchen, closing the door behind her. GEORGE answers the front door to CRICHTON.

CRICHTON: Mr Reynolds?

GEORGE: Yes.

CRICHTON: I assumed that must be your car. Obviously you found the place alright?

GEORGE: Yes, thank you. Your directions were very clear.

CRICHTON comes in and GEORGE closes the door behind him.

CRICHTON: I thought since I was early I might have a bit of a wait before you arrived.

GEORGE: No, I was early too. The drive didn't take as long as I expected.

CRICHTON: I see. Well I hope I haven't kept you waiting too long?

GEORGE: No, I've only been here a few minutes.

CRICHTON: Well, that is fortunate. And obviously the lady from the letting agency remembered to leave the key under the mat?

GEORGE: She did, yes. Imagine doing that in London, eh? It really is a different world out here. I guess they don't have to worry about crime.

CRICHTON: So you might think, sir, so you might think. In my experience, that's no more than a myth. I seem to recall there's a Sherlock Holmes story where they talk about this very subject. They're on a train to the countryside to investigate some case, and Watson remarks that he can't imagine anything bad happening in such a beautiful place. Holmes replies that even in the vilest back alley of London, there's a limit to human wickedness simply because people behave better when they know they might be observed by others. Out in the countryside, pretty though it may be, that safeguard doesn't exist. Especially in such a remote spot as this. *(Smiles.)* Not that I'm casting myself as Sherlock Holmes, of course. *(Slight pause.)* Or you as Dr Watson.

Beat.

Anyway, as I told you on the phone, my name's Detective Inspector Crichton, and I'm with the East Sussex County Constabulary… *(He notices GEORGE's mug with surprise.)* Is that tea you have there, sir?

GEORGE: *(Caught off guard.)* Oh…yes I…found it in the cupboard. The last people to rent the place must have left it behind. Seems alright, anyway. I guess tea doesn't really go off, does it?

CRICHTON: That's uncommonly handy. I always think a nice cup of tea really sets you up for the day. Unfortunately I didn't have time for one before I left home.

Beat.

GEORGE: *(Uncomfortably.)* Would you…like one now?

CRICHTON: That's very kind of you, sir.

GEORGE heads towards the kitchen.

GEORGE: There's no milk of course.

CRICHTON: *(Disappointed.)* Oh. No, I suppose there wouldn't be. Well, don't worry about it then. I don't like it without milk.

GEORGE: *(Trying to hide his relief.)* Fair enough. Well, do sit down.

CRICHTON's face registers surprise.

CRICHTON: Thank you, sir, I will.

He sits down on the sofa, GEORGE in the armchair.

GEORGE: So what was it you wanted to talk to me about?

CRICHTON: I'm investigating the murder of a Mr John Small. Is that name familiar to you at all, sir?

GEORGE: *(Considers.)* John Small…no, I don't think I knew him.

CRICHTON: *(His interest piqued.)* Now, that is interesting. Would you mind telling me why you just referred to him using the past tense?

GEORGE: You just told me he'd been murdered.

CRICHTON: *(With rueful amusement.)* So I did, sir, so I did. I hoped for a moment you'd saved me the trouble of what looks like being a rather tricky investigation.

GEORGE: Sorry to disappoint you.

CRICHTON: No matter, sir, no matter. To be honest, that sort of thing's only in detective stories. Never known it to happen in reality.

GEORGE: That sort of thing?

CRICHTON: Someone giving himself away by carelessly revealing that he knows more about the crime than he should. Like, for example, if you'd said 'It wasn't me that shot him' when I'd only told you Small had been killed, not that he'd been shot. Though he was, as it happens.

Shot. Right in this very room. We found him lying *(He indicates.)* just over there.

CRICHTON gets up to show exactly where the body was lying.

CRICHTON: The phone was lying just next to his outstretched hand. It seems he managed to get to the phone, dial 999 and ask for the police, but unfortunately died before he could say any more.

GEORGE: Now *that* sounds like something from a detective story.

CRICHTON sits down again.

CRICHTON: Doesn't it just. This was the evening of Thursday 13th January, about a month ago. He'd rented this place for a week, and was killed the very first night. Not quite so idyllic in the countryside as you thought, eh sir?

GEORGE doesn't answer.

CRICHTON: At first it seemed a pretty open and shut case. Small was a petty criminal with a string of minor offences to his credit, if that's the word. He also had gangland connections, which is never a recipe for a long and peaceful life. Then all of a sudden, he rents this place in the middle of nowhere. First person to rent it in months, they said, January not being exactly their busy season. *(Slight pause.)* Come to think of it, he must have bought that tea you're drinking.

GEORGE, who was just lifting the mug to his lips, pauses awkwardly, then puts the cup down again.

GEORGE: Dead man's tea.

CRICHTON: Quite. Anyway, it was clear that, for whatever reason, Small saw trouble coming and decided to lie low for a while. The fact that he only rented it for a week suggests he intended to keep moving, never staying in the same place for too long. But it seemed that whoever was after him managed to track him down. You see, the killing had all the hallmarks of a professional execution – a single shot to the heart at close range. Simple, neat, efficient. Just the way the criminal underworld might deal with one of their own.

GEORGE: Look, this is all very interesting, but can I ask why you wanted me to come all this way just to tell me this? I've told you I didn't know the man.

CRICHTON: I just thought that being here might help to…jog your memory a little.

GEORGE: *(Taken aback.)* Jog my memory?

CRICHTON: That's what I said, sir.

GEORGE: *(Astonished.)* You can't be implying…

CRICHTON: Oh I never imply, sir. Implication is not a weapon found in my verbal armoury.

GEORGE: *(Annoyed.)* Well whatever you want to call it, you can't seriously think I might have killed this John Small – no, hang on, I can say 'shot', can't I, since you've told me he was, so that's alright – you think I might have shot him a month ago and forgotten all about it until I saw this room again?

CRICHTON: *(Calmly.)* Oh, you'd be amazed what people forget, sir. I'm forever interviewing suspects who initially have no memory at all of something they later turn out to remember in every detail. The human memory is a strange and wond'rous thing.

GEORGE: *(Acidly.)* Well congratulations, Inspector, you're absolutely right. As soon as I walked in the door I went *(Slaps forehead.)* 'Hang on, didn't I shoot someone here a month ago? I thought the address sounded familiar.' Lucky for me you weren't here at the time, really. I mean, a detective of your calibre would probably have picked up on it.

CRICHTON: Very droll, sir. *(Slight pause.)* Incidentally, you don't need to keep referring to him as 'this John Small'. Just telling me once that you didn't know him is enough. Labouring the point actually makes me less inclined to believe it. Also, I can't help but notice that you do seem to feel very at home here for someone who arrived just a few minutes before I did. Making yourself tea, inviting me to sit down…

GEORGE: *(With annoyance.)* Well I'm sorry to disappoint you, but I haven't been here before, I didn't know him, and I wasn't sent by some mafia don to rub him out, as I believe is the term. At least, I don't think so, but when you kill as many people as I do, what with settling private grudges on top of my career as a professional hit man, they do tend to blur into one after a while…

CRICHTON: *(Calmly.)* There's no need to get overexcited, sir. We don't want any tears before bedtime, now do we? I only said that a professional hit was how it seemed *at first.* As it happens, that's not what we believe now. *(Slight pause.)* You see, sir, there were certain inconsistencies to that theory that a detective… *of my calibre* could hardly fail to pick up on. And I'm just not a man who can ignore a loose thread. I have a strange compulsion to tug at it and see what unravels.

Beat.

GEORGE: *(Calmer.)* So what was it? Your loose thread?

CRICHTON: Actually there were two. Firstly, I was always bothered by the fact that there was no sign of a forced entry. I mean, why go to all this trouble to hide away, and then cheerfully answer the door to the first person who knocks? In other words, his killer must have been someone he knew and trusted. Or at least someone he was expecting.

GEORGE: Fair point. What else?

CRICHTON: Well, it was a very trivial thing. Nine times out of ten it would have meant nothing, but some instinct told me it was worth pursuing. You see, the security cameras at an internet cafe near where Small lived in Penge recorded him making several visits in the month before he was killed. Nothing suspicious in that, except that he had a computer with an internet connection at home. We checked, and it was working perfectly. So I got to thinking, why would he bother going to an internet cafe when his computer at home was only a few minutes away?

There was only one possible answer. Whatever he was doing, he didn't want it traced back to him.

GEORGE: What, dodgy websites you mean?

CRICHTON: Hardly, sir. One doesn't do that sort of thing in public. Especially in Penge. So we examined the footage to determine which computers he'd used and at what times, and from this I – or rather, some more technically-minded people back at the station – were able to determine that what he was doing was sending emails. Though curiously, he wasn't sending them in his own name. Do you know what name he was using, sir?

GEORGE: *(Irritably.)* Of course I don't. How could I possibly know?

CRICHTON: *(Slowly and clearly.)* 'Old Acquaintance'.

GEORGE: Old Acquaintance?

CRICHTON: Yes, sir.

GEORGE: As in 'Should old acquaintance be forgot'?

CRICHTON: Quite possibly, sir. You see, the curious thing was that he used this email account to write to only one person, a Miss Charlotte Chamberlain. Perhaps you know her, sir?

GEORGE: No, I can't say I do.

CRICHTON: But you have heard of the Chamberlain family?

GEORGE: Oh, you mean *the* Chamberlains? Well I've heard of them, of course. *(Thinks.)* Charlotte's the daughter, isn't she?

CRICHTON: That's right, sir. Described in a recent edition of *Hello!* magazine as a *(Reading from his notes.)* 'wealthy heiress and glamorous socialist'. *(Taken aback.)* Hang on, that can't be right…

GEORGE: 'Socialite' perhaps?

CRICHTON: *(With wry amusement.)* Yes, that does seem a bit more likely, doesn't it? Apparently her life is an endless round of parties and other social events, with the occasional skiing holiday thrown in just for variety.

GEORGE: Nice work if you can get it.

CRICHTON: Quite. Which makes it rather unlikely that she and Small would know each other, don't you think?

GEORGE: Yes… *(Catches himself.)* from what you've said about him.

CRICHTON: So as you can imagine, I was very curious to see what the emails said. But nothing could have prepared me for the shock when I read them.

GEORGE: Why, what did they say?

CRICHTON: Blackmail, sir.

GEORGE: He was blackmailing her?

CRICHTON: Yes, sir.

GEORGE: About what?

CRICHTON: We don't know. The emails keep it very vague, deliberately so in my opinion. He just says he knows her guilty secret, and demands money in return for keeping quiet about it. I suppose he assumed she'd know what he was talking about, so he didn't need to spell it out. What it is, we've no idea.

GEORGE: I see.

CRICHTON: Of course, it could have been that he didn't know anything about her except that she's wealthy, and was just trying his luck – hoping that if she *did* have something to hide, she'd panic and pay up rather than risk calling his bluff. Fishing, it's called. People have been known to do that.

GEORGE: That would explain the vagueness, I suppose. How did she respond?

CRICHTON: She didn't reply to any of his emails.

GEORGE: Well, presumably as you say he didn't really have anything on her.

CRICHTON: That's what I would have thought, if not for the fact that he didn't send similar emails to anyone else, only to her. After all, there are plenty of rich people in the world. Why choose her if not because she *did* have something to hide, and he'd somehow found out about it?

Beat.

CRICHTON: Anyway, as it happens the question was resolved by the last email. In it he tells Miss Chamberlain in no uncertain terms to bring the payment to this address.

GEORGE: *(Apparently surprised.)* Here?

CRICHTON: That's right, sir. He gave her very detailed directions. The same ones I gave you, in fact. He told her to be here at nine that evening, or else he'd go public with what he knew. This was about a month ago. The night he was killed.

GEORGE: What, and you think *she...* *(He tails off.)*

CRICHTON: Indeed sir. It does rather look as if she killed him to keep him quiet.

GEORGE: But why wouldn't she just pay him off? She could afford to, surely.

CRICHTON: Perhaps she was worried he wouldn't keep his side of the bargain. That's almost always the case with blackmailers, they don't give up the hold they have over you without a fight. Then again, perhaps she simply didn't have the money. After all, it's her father who's rich, not her, and maybe this wasn't something she could go to him about. *(Slight pause.)* For all we know, he might be the very person the secret had to be kept from.

Beat.

CRICHTON: Of course, I'm not pretending it's going to be easy to prove any of this. There's little chance of us ever finding the gun – she's had plenty of time to dispose of it. And we didn't find any fingerprints to prove she was ever here.

63

GEORGE: What about DNA evidence?

CRICHTON: *(Amused.)* DNA evidence. Been watching a bit of telly, have we sir?

GEORGE: Well, I just thought...

CRICHTON: I'm with the East Sussex County Constabulary, not CSI New York. We only got a microwave in the canteen two months ago. *(Slight pause.)* Anyway, with or without proof you have to admit that, as a working hypothesis, it does explain a lot – Small's sudden desire to rent this remote farmhouse in the middle of winter, and why he answered the door to his killer. He assumed she was there to pay him off. *(Slight pause.)* In any case, what's the alternative? That someone she had every reason to want dead told her to meet him here at nine that evening, threatening to ruin her if she didn't, she inexplicably didn't bother to go, and then he was killed here at nine that evening in a completely unrelated incident? Bit of a coincidence, wouldn't you say?

GEORGE: I suppose...it's just hard to believe that someone in her position would risk throwing it all away like that.

CRICHTON: Who can say, sir? I suppose it depends on what Small knew about her. And that, as I say, we don't know. If it were damaging enough, she might do anything to keep it a secret.

GEORGE: But even if she did want him killed, surely she wouldn't risk doing it herself?

CRICHTON: Maybe she thought involving a third party was more of a risk. Then again, maybe she just didn't have time. Small sent the email at midday, and told her to be here at nine. Not much time to find a professional killer, unless you're lucky enough to have one among your personal acquaintances.

GEORGE: I suppose not. What does she say about it all?

CRICHTON: We haven't questioned her yet, sir. With a family like that, you don't want to go barging in making accusations until you've exhausted every other line of enquiry. *(Wryly.)* After all, you never know who plays golf with the Chief Super.

GEORGE: I'm sure.

CRICHTON: And that, sir, is where you come in.

GEORGE: *(Taken aback.)* Me? I still don't see what any of this has to do with me.

CRICHTON: Well, sir, there's just one thing that still puzzles me about this case. One piece that won't quite fit into place.

GEORGE: What's that?

CRICHTON: *(Picks up phone.)* Two phone calls were made from this phone to your flat at around the time Small was killed.

Beat.

GEORGE: Really?

CRICHTON: Yes, sir. *(Consults notebook.)* One at 8.51, one at 9.07. Naturally I find this rather puzzling, since you've repeatedly told me you didn't know the man.

GEORGE, his wheels turning furiously, doesn't respond.

CRICHTON: Each call lasted several minutes, which would seem to rule out a wrong number. Especially since the same number was dialled twice.

GEORGE: Can I ask why you didn't mention this before?

CRICHTON: A new directive from Brussels, sir. We have to start by telling suspects everything we know about a case. Gives them a sporting chance to come up with a story that accounts for all the known facts, but still leaves them in the clear.

GEORGE: *(Surprised.)* Really?

CRICHTON gives him a withering look.

GEORGE: *(Embarrassed.)* No. Of course not.

CRICHTON: So, about these phone calls. Can you account for them, sir?

GEORGE: No. I just can't understand it.

CRICHTON: No one else lives there with you, I believe?

GEORGE: No…a Thursday night about a month ago, you say? Two phone calls from the same number, about fifteen minutes apart…

CRICHTON: That's right, sir.

GEORGE: Oh hang on. Maybe…yes of course, that must be it.

CRICHTON: *(Drily.)* All coming back to you now, is it sir?

GEORGE: *(Too quickly.)* You see, I didn't know him as John Small. That's why I didn't recognise the name. He used a different name with me. And no wonder. I mean, you'd expect him to be using false names if he was mixed up in the kind of thing you say he was. *(With forced jollity.)* You know what he told me his name was? You'll never believe it.

CRICHTON: *(Drily.)* We shall just have to take that risk, sir.

GEORGE: John Little. How about that?

CRICHTON: *(Wearily.)* Anyway, false name notwithstanding, you're admitting that you did know him?

GEORGE: Well, I didn't know him exactly. He was an odd job man who'd done a few jobs for me around the house. Electrics, plumbing, that sort of thing.

CRICHTON: I see. And would you mind telling me what you talked about when he called you that night?

GEORGE: Yes, I remember now. He was after a reference. He was going for a job as a maintenance man for an upmarket block of flats, and they wanted references from his previous clients.

CRICHTON: And you were happy to provide one?

GEORGE: No. I'd found his work very careless. I'd already decided not to use him again. When he asked for a reference, I refused and told him why. That's why he called back a bit later – to try and change my mind.

CRICHTON: *(Wearily.)* Mr Reynolds, are you seriously telling me that Small, who told you his name was Little – and no doubt told the next three people he met that it was Tiny, Petite and Miniscule – that this man who believed he was about to make a fortune from a blackmail scheme, called you not once but twice in pursuit of a reference to help him get a job as a *caretaker*?

GEORGE: Well I don't know anything about any blackmail. Or what his real name was. All I know is that…

CRICHTON: *(Wearily.)* Shall I tell you what I think, sir? It might save time.

GEORGE does not respond.

CRICHTON: At first, it seemed clear enough. I was certain that you *did* after all know *this* John Small. In fact, I was pretty certain you were the brains behind the blackmail scheme. That made perfect sense, since by all accounts Small wasn't the sharpest tool in the box. In fact, as one of his neighbours rather colourfully put it, he'd have had trouble pouring piss out of a boot that had the instructions printed on the heel. No, it seemed to me much more likely that *you* found out Miss Chamberlain's guilty secret, whatever it is, decided to blackmail her, and got Small to be your front man in exchange for a share of the money. That way, if anything went wrong, he'd take the blame and you'd be in the clear. When you found out she'd killed him, you simply cut your losses and moved on.

But then, a more intriguing possibility occurred to me.

GEORGE: *(Archly.)* I can hardly wait.

CRICHTON: I thought to myself, what if it wasn't Small who phoned you? What if it was Miss Chamberlain?

GEORGE: Why would she call me? I've told you I don't know her.

CRICHTON: *(Smiles.)* That you have, sir, and best of all you only said it once. I'm glad to see my pearls of wisdom aren't falling on stony ground, if you'll forgive the mixed metaphor. But then you also said you didn't know Small, so what am I to believe?

GEORGE: *(Annoyed.)* Look, I've explained about that...

CRICHTON: *(Interrupting.)* You see, sir, what I was thinking was this. She brings a gun, hoping to scare Small into backing down, but things get out of hand and she shoots him dead. Naturally she's in a state of panic, so who does she turn to but her old friend Mr Reynolds. He's a man of the world, he'll know what to do. She can't get a signal on her mobile, out here in the middle of nowhere, so she's forced to use the landline, not realising in her panic that she's incriminating you by doing so. And good old Mr Reynolds, unflappable as ever, comes up trumps. You tell her to wipe down anything she's touched and throw the gun in the river. The police may still find it, of course, and match it to the bullet that killed Small, but so what? There'll be nothing to link it to her. *(With a smile.)* Not even DNA evidence. She calls you again to say she's done it. Perhaps that's when you gave her the idea of dialing 999 and leaving the phone by his hand, as if he made the call himself just before dying.

CRICHTON sits forward.

CRICHTON: So the question I'm asking myself is, which one of them were you in league with? In other words, are you an accessory to blackmail, or to murder?

Beat.

CRICHTON: For what it's worth, my money's on blackmail. You see, I recently learned that certain colleagues of mine have been called in to investigate a case of industrial espionage at her father's company, Chamberlain Industries. It seems some extremely valuable information has somehow leaked out. Something to do with a new invention of some kind. Information so sensitive that only a handful of people had access to it.

And that's when I realised that the payoff Small was demanding wasn't money at all. He wanted valuable information which Miss Chamberlain, as a director of the company, would be able to get him.

GEORGE: But…why would she steal this information to pay him off, and then kill him?

CRICHTON: As I said, maybe she brought the gun to frighten him, but things got out of hand. Or maybe she just decided she couldn't trust him to keep his end of the bargain. The point is, it puts it beyond any doubt that Small wasn't the brains of the operation. I could just about believe him capable of demanding money with crude threats. But obtaining complex technical information, finding a buyer, convincing them the information was genuine, negotiating a price and so forth? Oh no, sir. That had to someone else. *(Sarcastically.)* Now, who could that other person be, I wonder? Could it perhaps be the person he phoned twice around the time when, as he thought, she was about to bring him the information?

Beat.

But who knows, maybe I'm wrong. No matter. We'll have plenty of time to fill in the blanks back at the station.

GEORGE: *(Surprised.)* What?

CRICHTON: Well, how did you think our little chat was going to end? Obviously I'm going to ask you to accompany me back to the station, so we can get to the bottom of your involvement in this business.

GEORGE: What am I being charged with?

CRICHTON: Nothing yet, sir. But we have plenty of time to decide. If you watch the news, you'll be aware that we can hold people without charge for quite a long time these days.

GEORGE: But…that's just in terrorism cases, surely?

CRICHTON: Well that's just it, sir. You can never tell at first sight whether a case is linked to terrorism. Not until you've investigated it thoroughly. Something that in my experience the layman entirely fails to understand. Even the most routine convenience store robbery might have been committed to raise funds for a terrorist network.

GEORGE: Really?

CRICHTON: Oh yes, sir. So you see, we have to approach every case on the assumption that it might, ultimately, be linked to terrorism. And if it turns out to be just a simple, isolated crime with no broader implications, well, we weren't to know, were we? Not until we'd completed the investigation. Sort of a Catch 22 situation, really. But given this uncertainty, I'm sure you'd agree we should err on the side of thoroughness?

GEORGE: But surely you can't just...

CRICHTON: *(Interrupting.)* Oh, don't misunderstand me, sir. I'm not talking about beatings and electric shocks. We're not the West Midlands police, after all.

Beat.

CRICHTON: That was a joke, sir.

GEORGE: *(Disconcerted.)* Oh. Yes.

CRICHTON: No, just good old-fashioned policework, that's all. Thorough, methodical and above all patient. *(He leans forward conspiratorially.)* If you ask me, sir, it's the food that breaks most people in the end. Though I can assure you it's just the same as we get in the staff canteen.

CRICHTON stands.

CRICHTON: Well, the sooner we start, the sooner we finish. If you wouldn't mind accompanying me to the station, sir. My car's just outside.

GEORGE: But...what about my car? I can't just leave it here.

CRICHTON: We'll send someone to take care of it.

GEORGE: *(In growing panic.)* Look, you're making a mistake.

CRICHTON: You'll have plenty of time to tell us your side of the story, sir. Now come along. Don't make this more difficult than it needs to be.

GEORGE: I can explain about the phone calls.

CRICHTON: *(Taking his arm.)* I look forward to hearing it, sir. I hope it's better than that story about your odd job man wanting a reference.

GEORGE: Take your hands off me…

There is a noise from the kitchen. Both men freeze looking in that direction.

CRICHTON: Is there someone here with you, sir?

GEORGE: No.

CRICHTON: Then how would you account for that noise?

Beat.

GEORGE: Mice?

CRICHTON gives GEORGE a withering look. He lets go of his arm and walks over to the kitchen door.

CRICHTON: Hello? Someone in there?

No reply.

CRICHTON: I'd advise you to come out. I would open the door myself, only I don't know where you're standing, and I'm concerned it might hit you and leave you with a nasty bruise, and you wouldn't believe how much extra paperwork that generates.

The kitchen door opens slowly. CHARLOTTE emerges, looking terrified. She is not carrying her bag.

CRICHTON: *(Taken aback.)* Well, well, well. Charlotte Chamberlain, I presume. And what brings you to this part of the world? Some local gymkhana, I expect?

She doesn't answer.

CRICHTON: *(To GEORGE.)* I suppose this answers my question. Too bad. Accessory to blackmail carries a much shorter sentence than accessory to murder. *(To CHARLOTTE.)* I take it you heard our conversation?

CHARLOTTE: The serving hatch was open. *(Desperately.)* Look, this isn't how it seems…

CRICHTON: You'll get your chance to make a statement back at the station. Only I hope you two have got your stories straight already, because you won't have a chance to confer from here on. To which end, I'd better call for second car to take you in.

He takes out a walkie-talkie.

CRICHTON: DI Crichton to Control.

A crackle of static, then no response.

CRICHTON: Control, this is DI Crichton.

The same.

CRICHTON: Must be a dead spot.

He puts the walkie-talkie away ponders a moment.

CRICHTON: Right, here's what we'll do. Miss Chamberlain, you come with me. I'm not leaving you two alone together. If I drive back to the main road, I should be able to call it in from there. Mr Reynolds, you wait here, we should only be a few minutes. In the meantime, forgive my suspicious nature, but I'll take your car keys with me if you don't mind.

GEORGE reluctantly digs out his car keys and gives them to CRICHTON.

CRICHTON: I need hardly add that trying to make a break for it on foot would be entirely pointless. You're right in the middle of nowhere. You wouldn't get away, and it wouldn't look good if you tried to run for it. It's just the sort of thing that makes juries jump to conclusions.

GEORGE says nothing.

CRICHTON: Well, until we meet again, Mr Reynolds. Come along, Miss Chamberlain.

CRICHTON and CHARLOTTE leave through the front door. We hear a car start and drive away. GEORGE watches from the window. He paces around the room. He looks in annoyance at the phone. With nothing else to do, he sits down again in the armchair. Again his wheels are turning furiously – how can he get out of this? Suddenly there is the sound of running footsteps and a hammering at the front door. Surprised, GEORGE answers it. It is CHARLOTTE, out of breath, holding her high-heels in one hand.

GEORGE: *(Surprised.)* Miss Chamberlain!

CHARLOTTE: *(Frantically.)* Quickly, my bag! Where is it?

GEORGE: *(Looking around.)* Er…it must be in the kitchen.

CHARLOTTE rushes into the kitchen.

GEORGE: *(Closing the door.)* How the hell did you get away from him?

CHARLOTTE returns with the bag, dumps it on the table and starts furiously rooting through it.

CHARLOTTE: He had to stop to open the gate at the end of the lane. I took my chance and made a run for it. But we haven't got long, he'll be back here any minute.

GEORGE: Well, what the hell are we going to do? He's got my car keys.

CHARLOTTE: He didn't take mine. They're in here somewhere.

GEORGE: Anyway, that's the only road away from here.

CHARLOTTE: We can go across the fields. My car's a 4 x 4.

GEORGE: *(Drily.)* Of course it is. But even if we do get away, what are we supposed to do then?

CHARLOTTE: *(Irritated.)* I don't bloody know. If you'd rather just stay here and be arrested, be my guest.

GEORGE: He knows who we are.

CHARLOTTE: I'm well aware of that.

GEORGE: We can't just keep running forever.

CHARLOTTE: *(Sarcastically.)* Oh it's *we* now, is it? Now you need my help?

GEORGE: Like it or not, we're in this together. I've got the evidence against you. If I go down, you go down.

CHARLOTTE: I can be out of the country in a couple of hours.

GEORGE: There is such a thing as extradition.

CHARLOTTE: There's also such a thing as high-priced lawyers who can delay the process indefinitely.

She continues rooting through the bag.

GEORGE: *(Nervously.)* Look, have you got those bloody keys or not?

CHARLOTTE: Give me a minute!

GEORGE glances nervously out of the window.

GEORGE: For God's sake!

CHARLOTTE: *(Pushing the bag at him.)* Well, you find them then!

GEORGE: All right, but you keep watch. Let me know the moment you see him.

CHARLOTTE goes to the window and looks out. GEORGE frantically roots through her bag.

GEORGE: Honestly, the amount of crap you women keep in these bags. You do realise you can lock your front door? You don't have to take everything you own with you every time you leave the house?

CHARLOTTE: *(Suddenly alarmed.)* He's coming! Hurry up!

GEORGE: Are you sure they're in here?

CHARLOTTE: Of course I am. Try in the pockets. Quickly!

GEORGE starts pulling everything out of the bag and piling it on the table. General woman's handbag stuff.

GEORGE: I suppose there's no way you women could just put things in the same place every time? So it didn't always take half an hour to find anything? That would be too much to ask, wouldn't it?

There is a firm knock at the door.

GEORGE: Don't answer it!

CHARLOTTE: *(Sarcastically.)* Sure, maybe if we keep really quiet he'll think we're not at home and go away.

She starts to walk towards the door. There is another, firmer knock.

GEORGE: Just give me a minute!

CHARLOTTE: It's too late, George.

CHARLOTTE opens the door to admit JOHN. He looks just as he did as LENNIE in Act One and still speaks with an East-End accent, though now with a more confident, articulate tone. He is wearing gloves.

GEORGE, still holding CHARLOTTE's bag, wheels round to face, as he assumes, CRICHTON. Seeing who it really is horrifies him far more. He stares. His mouth opens and closes but his voice won't work.

JOHN: *(In mock reproach.)* Oh Mr R – not with those shoes.

GEORGE realises he is still holding the handbag. CHARLOTTE takes her car keys out of her pocket.

CHARLOTTE: Well look at that, they were in my pocket all the time. Us women, eh? What are we like? *(To JOHN, happily.)* Hello darling.

She kisses him passionately.

JOHN: Easy love, don't give him too many shocks at once. He's not as young as he was.

GEORGE continues to look between them in silent consternation.

JOHN: You're looking a little bewildered, George. Let's see if I can make things clearer for you. In Mark Twain's famous phrase, reports of my death were greatly exaggerated. But of course, you're more of a Steinbeck man, aren't you?

GEORGE: But you…it's not possible…

JOHN: What, you think we're an unlikely couple? Well that's charming, isn't it?

CHARLOTTE: And this from the man who insists that social position is just an accident of birth.

JOHN: Though in fairness we should admit that your father would agree.

CHARLOTTE: Hmm, sadly that is true.

GEORGE: *(In desperation.)* Look…just what the hell is going on?

JOHN: A reasonable question, in the circumstances. Well, it's like this.

(He clears his throat and declaims, an old-fashioned Shakespearean ham.)

'Two households, both alike in dignity,
In fair Verona, where we lay our scene,
A pair of star-cross'd lovers…'

CHARLOTTE: *(Admonishing him playfully.)* John! Can't you take anything seriously? Star-cross'd lovers…

JOHN: *(Cheerfully.)* Well, what else would you call us? But if you insist on being so mundane, let's just say that Charlie's dad would never agree to us getting married. Truth is, our households aren't exactly alike in dignity – her dad's a multi-millionaire industrialist, and mine's a bus driver. So there's every chance of Charlie ending up potless if she ignores her father's wishes and marries me. *(With great nobility.)* And I would *never* ask her to make that sacrifice. *(Drily.)* Especially when it screws up my future as well.

She cuffs him playfully.

JOHN: What we needed was some money of our own, and who better to give it to us than daddy dearest? But how to loosen the strings of that jealously-guarded purse? *(Muses.)* Hmmm… What if he thought his darling daughter, the apple of his proverbial, had been kidnapped? That should do it. He'd pay a fortune to get her back.

GEORGE's face registers astonishment.

CHARLOTTE: *(Sarcastically.)* Oh I'm sorry, did you think that was your idea? 'Fraid not. Mine and John's. You were just the puppet, the frontman so John never had to speak to daddy himself.

JOHN: But then the puppet started to make plans of its own, didn't it? Started getting ideas above its station. I mean, why send threatening emails to someone you're about to kidnap? Even Lennie could have told you that didn't add up. And why give me a gun with only one bullet?

Obviously someone was in for a nasty surprise. But killing Charlie didn't make any sense – we'd never get a penny out of her dad, and he'd hunt us down to the ends of the earth. So unless the whole thing was an elaborate suicide attempt on your part, that bullet had to be meant for me. You were relying on Charlie to get hold of the gun and shoot me while trying to escape.

Not nice, George, really not nice. I mean, if you didn't wanna share the loot, you might at least have the balls to do your own dirty work. But then the penny dropped – it wasn't just about getting me out the way, was it? Those emails you got me to send her would make it look as if she'd killed me to keep me quiet. Very clever. For the life of me, I couldn't work out why you assumed she had a guilty secret to hide. But you weren't assuming she did, you were making damn sure she did – the cold-blooded murder of blackmailer John Small. Ever since that night in the Six Bells when I came to you with the kidnap plan, you'd been plotting to turn it into this grand scheme that ended up with me dead and her in the frame for it. Then she'd be right in your power.

But I can't help wondering, how were you planning to make sure she did it? You couldn't have been certain she'd get the gun off me, surely? You must have had a backup plan… A knife from the kitchen drawer? *(Indicates an old farm implement mounted on the wall.)* The scythe off the wall? The candlestick in the library?

GEORGE doesn't answer. An sudden realisation strikes JOHN.

JOHN: Of course, how stupid of me. It didn't matter if she didn't kill me, did it? You could do it yourself, just so long as you got her prints on the murder weapon. That was your fallback.

Beat.

JOHN: *(Considers.)* Hmm. It's all a bit wing-and-a-prayer, if you don't mind a little constructive criticism. Too much left to chance. *(To CHARLOTTE.)* Frankly I think it's just as well we took charge.

GEORGE: *(Astonished.)* You?

CHARLOTTE: Of course. We could have just called the whole thing off when we realised what you were up to, but then we'd be back to square one, with no money or prospect of getting any. So we decided to go through with it. *(Drily.)* With a couple of tiny changes, of course.

JOHN: Replacing the live round with a blank. Fake blood inside my shirt.

GEORGE: *(Baffled.)* But... I heard you. *(To CHARLOTTE.)* You were begging him to help you escape.

CHARLOTTE: Don't be an idiot, George, it was all for your benefit. We knew perfectly well you were listening in.

GEORGE: *(Clutching at straws.)* But... Inspector Crichton... *(To JOHN.)* He said they found your body...

JOHN: Ah yes, 'the admirable Crichton'. Though his name's really Moncrieff.

GEORGE: Moncrieff?

CHARLOTTE: Our butler.

GEORGE: *What?*

CHARLOTTE: You do know *The Admirable Crichton*, don't you George? By J.M. Barrie? I did it for A-level. Basically it's all about this butler who's incredibly resourceful, able to turn his hand to anything, solve any problem. Rather like our own Moncrieff, come to think of it. Still, it must have made a nice change from laying out the cutlery. *(Slight pause.)* The trick, by the way, is to work inwards.

GEORGE: What?

CHARLOTTE: With knives and forks. You start from the outside and work inwards.

GEORGE says nothing.

CHARLOTTE: Oh cheer up, Mr Reynolds, surely you don't begrudge us a bit of fun? Anyway, this is good news for you. You're not going to be arrested as an accessory to blackmail, murder or anything else. Surely you're happy about that? Oh, speaking of accessories, pass me my bag would you?

GEORGE dumbly passes it to her. She sits down on the sofa and starts replacing everything in it.

CHARLOTTE: D'you know, I think I will have that tea after all, if your offer still stands. *(To JOHN.)* How about you, darling?

JOHN sits next to her.

JOHN: Tea'd be smashing, thanks. You remember how I like it, Mr R? I know, so much sugar's bad for me, but what the hell, I'll risk it.

GEORGE is staring into the middle distance, his wheels turning furiously. During the following exchange he becomes more and more alarmed.

JOHN: *(To CHARLOTTE.)* Hmm. Doesn't look very happy, does he? Why's that, d'you reckon?

CHARLOTTE: *(To JOHN.)* D'you know, I bet he's just realised that since you're not dead, he's got no hold over me at all.

JOHN: Very true. Without a dead body, who cares about a gun with your prints on it?

CHARLOTTE: Which means I can tell Daddy *all* about him.

JOHN: The kidnapping, the blackmail…

CHARLOTTE: He's been extorting money out of Daddy too, did you know that?

JOHN: He never!

CHARLOTTE: Anonymously, of course, he's not stupid. Twenty million or he'd sell the Omega plans to one of his competitors.

JOHN: Well, the cheeky little scamp. Don't tell me your dad paid up?

CHARLOTTE: Had to. Couldn't take the risk.

JOHN: I can imagine how much he enjoyed that.

CHARLOTTE: Oh, he was livid.

JOHN: Let's hope he never finds out who it was…

GEORGE: *(Blurts out.)* Look, I'll…give you money.

Beat. They both look at him.

JOHN: Sorry, did you say something?

GEORGE: You need money, you said so yourself. I'll split the twenty million with you.

CHARLOTTE: What, you get ten and we split the other ten between us? You must be joking.

GEORGE: All right, three ways.

CHARLOTTE: You can count yourself damn lucky if we let you keep any of it.

JOHN: Anyway we don't need your money. As it happens, a little scheme of our own has just paid off very handsomely. You see, while Charlie was giving you the Omega plans, I was giving them to Ziemann Industries, Chamberlain's main competitor. Like you said, they paid ten million for them. They got straight to work, and a couple of days ago they were officially informed they'd been granted the patent. Imagine when her dad finds out, eh? All those years he spent working on it, and now someone else is going to make all the money that's rightfully his. *(To CHARLOTTE, as if piecing it all together.)* Hang on a mo – didn't you just say George threatened to sell the plans to one of your dad's competitors?

CHARLOTTE: He did, yes.

JOHN: And now one of his competitors has somehow got hold of the plans.

CHARLOTTE: Seems that way.

JOHN: You don't think your dad might jump to the conclusion…

CHARLOTTE: D'you know, he just might…

GEORGE: *(Panicked.)* All right, you can have it all. Twenty million. Just don't tell him who I am.

JOHN: You're not listening, George. We don't want your money. *(With relish.)* What's about to happen to you is all the reward I need.

GEORGE: *(Desperate.)* Please!

JOHN: Then again, maybe we should do it the traditional way, leave you alone with a bottle of scotch and a revolver – and of course a single bullet. Give you a chance to do the honourable thing. It's certainly preferable to what'll happen when Chamberlain catches up with you.

CHARLOTTE: *(Admonishing him.)* Darling.

JOHN: What?

CHARLOTTE: This is my father you're talking about.

JOHN: I'm not saying he'd be personally involved. Just, er, associates of his. Old friends who owed him a favour.

CHARLOTTE: But ultimately he'd be behind it? Is that what you're saying?

JOHN: Look, you can't honestly be telling me you didn't know.

CHARLOTTE: *(Annoyed.)* The idea was to frighten him. You always have to take everything too far.

JOHN: *Too far?* Have you forgotten that if he had his way, I'd be dead and you'd be facing life in prison?

CHARLOTTE: Of course I haven't, but that's not the point.

JOHN: So what is the point?

CHARLOTTE: If we behave the way he does, then we're no better than him, are we?

JOHN: No better? He'll be dead and we'll be alive. Seems to me that's better.

CHARLOTTE: That's not what I mean. It's a matter of principle.

JOHN: Look, you might have been doing this for a jolly old wheeze, but I'm out for revenge, pure and simple. Where I come from, you don't let people disrespect you like that and get away with it.

CHARLOTTE: And have you considered what would actually happen if we told Daddy about him? What a can of worms we'd be opening? *How am I supposed to explain the fact that I gave him the plans when he didn't really have anything to blackmail me with?*

JOHN: So what was the point of planting all that evidence against him?

CHARLOTTE: To force him to give us the money, of course. I realise the ten million we've got probably seems like a fortune to you...

JOHN: *(Sharply.)* Don't patronise me.

CHARLOTTE: *(Placatory.)* I'm sorry, darling, I really didn't mean to. I'm just saying I'm used to this lifestyle. You might think ten million is more than you could ever spend, but it really isn't. Besides, if I am disinherited, ten million doesn't come close to covering what I'm giving up for you. Here's a chance to make sure we're set up for life. Surely that's worth more than some pointless act of revenge?

JOHN: I can't believe you're seriously thinking of trusting this man, after what he did to us.

CHARLOTTE: Trust doesn't come into it. He gives us the money or we tell Daddy about him.

JOHN: Which you've just pretty much admitted you wouldn't go through with anyway. Anyway, he can blackmail us too – he knows we tried to con your dad by faking the kidnapping. We'd spend the rest of our lives looking over our shoulders. And I'm just not prepared to take that risk.

He stands, pulls out a gun and points it at GEORGE, who is terrified. CHARLOTTE stands.

CHARLOTTE: *(Horrified.)* What the hell are you doing?

JOHN: What we came to do. If you won't go through with it, I will.

CHARLOTTE: *(Desperately.)* John, just stop and think for a minute. We can walk out of here with thirty million and the rest of our lives to spend it together. Don't throw all that away. Who cares what happens to him? *He's not that important.* Let's just take his money and walk away.

JOHN: It's not about the money. It's a matter of honour.

CHARLOTTE: *(Hysterical.)* Honour? John, I'm begging you, don't throw away everything we've…

JOHN suddenly turns the gun on CHARLOTTE and shoots her through the heart. She falls slowly to the ground, her eyes fixed on him the whole time. JOHN's expression does not change.

JOHN: Annoying when they go on like that, don't you think?

He walks calmly over to her body. He looks through her bag to find her compact, and holds the mirror next to her mouth.

JOHN: Thought for the day – if you wanna make sure someone's dead, you really need to check if they're still breathing. Just seeing a bloodstain doesn't prove anything.

GEORGE takes a step towards him. JOHN quickly covers him with the gun.

JOHN: Not so fast, Georgie boy. More than one bullet in the gun this time.

GEORGE: *(Grimly.)* No doubt.

JOHN: *(Amused.)* No, that's not what I meant. I've got no reason to kill you. *(Indicating the armchair with the gun.)* Do sit down, old boy. Take the weight off.

GEORGE sits down in the armchair.

GEORGE: Did you have any reason to kill *her*?

JOHN: *(Reflectively.)* I suppose I could have gone ahead with the whole marriage thing. Can't deny I was tempted. I don't know if you've found this, but a lot of times with good-looking birds, they don't really make much of an effort in bed. They think they're doing you such a huge favour just by being there. But not our Charlie. She really put body and soul into it. *(Smiles.)* Well, body anyway. So yeah, not an easy decision. But then I thought, I'm still a young man, and as of this morning, a young man with ten million in the bank. The world's my lobster, as Lennie might have put it. And like I was telling you, I do like to get a new model every year. Shallow, I suppose, but there you are.

GEORGE is silent.

JOHN: Anyway, truth is she knew too much about me. Sure, it was all very Mills and Boon now, but what if in a few years she's missing all the Ruperts and Sebastians and wants me out the way? I couldn't risk her going to the police with what she knew – or, even worse, going to Daddy. So I pointed out your little slip up, calling your own home number from this phone while there was supposedly a murder taking place here, and suggested she got the admirable Moncrieff to pose as a police inspector and put the wind up you. And she loved the idea, thought it was hilarious. Never even crossed her mind that my real motive was to get you both to an isolated spot at the same time.

Beat.

JOHN: But hark at me, banging on about meself when you must be wondering about your own future. Well, it seems to me you have a dead heiress on your hands. When news of this gets back to Chamberlain Towers, good old Moncrieff'll spill the beans about you, and the identity of the mystery blackmailer will finally be revealed. So let's see if I've got this straight *(He counts them off on his fingers.)* you blackmailed Charlie here to get you the plans, you blackmailed Daddy to pay you not to sell them on to his competitors, you double-crossed him and sold them on anyway, and now you've killed his daughter, presumably because she objected to one or more of the above. Didn't miss anything out, did I?

GEORGE: *Me?* I didn't kill her!

JOHN: Yeah, you should definitely mention that. Can't see anyone believing you, though. Not after the police find you alone here with the body...

GEORGE: *(Alarmed.)* What?

JOHN crosses to CHARLOTTE's body, starts looking through her pockets.

JOHN: Oh, didn't I mention? I had a look at your car just now, and it seems someone's let all the tyres down. Kids, I expect. What is the world coming to? I would give you a lift, but something tells me we're going in different directions.

JOHN stands up, CHARLOTTE's car keys in his hand.

JOHN: Did you know you can't disconnect a 999 call? Neither did I till that night. And the annoying thing is the police do insist on coming round, even if you say you don't need them and you only called them by accident. 'Spose they have to make sure you're not saying it with a gun to your head. Oh, which reminds me, I'd better leave you with the murder weapon.

JOHN puts the gun on the table. It is some distance away from GEORGE who stares at it, calculating his chances. JOHN walks over to the telephone.

JOHN: They can trace bullets back to the gun that fired them, did you know that? Terribly clever, those forensics boffins.

He turns round, receiver in hand, to find GEORGE has picked up the gun and is pointing it at him.

Beat.

JOHN: So what's it to be, George? Not so easy when you have to do it yourself, is it? When you haven't got some poor little rich girl to do your killing for you...

He is interrupted by GEORGE pulling the trigger. It only produces a gentle click. He tries again, and again. Just a gentle click each time.

JOHN: Hmm. Guess there was only one bullet after all. D'you know, that's twice you've tried to kill me now? A lesser man might take it personally. Me, I'm just happy you've left your fingerprints on the gun. Course, you can wipe them off before the police get here, if you like – doesn't really make any difference. Now, where was I?

He dials 999.

JOHN: *(Into phone.)* Police.

He tosses the phone to GEORGE, who catches it instinctively, dropping the gun as he does so. JOHN walks to the front door, opens it and leaves, waving goodbye with a cheery smile and closing the door behind him. GEORGE stares dumbly after him, then sits down in the chair, phone still in his hand. After a moment we hear the car door open and close, then the engine turns over but does not catch. He tries again, with the same result. GEORGE starts to laugh. His laughter becomes manic and uncontrollable as we hear JOHN trying the engine for a third and then a fourth time.

End of play.

WWW.OBERONBOOKS.COM

Follow us on www.twitter.com/@oberonbooks
& www.facebook.com/oberonbook

www.ingramcontent.com/pod-product-compliance
Ingram Content Group UK Ltd.
Pitfield, Milton Keynes, MK11 3LW, UK
UKHW020725280225
455688UK00012B/509